the
home color selector

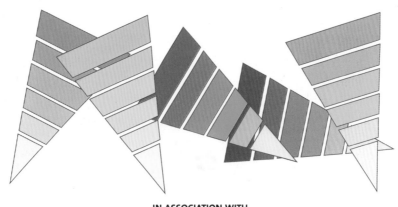

IN ASSOCIATION WITH

Benjamin Moore®
Paints

M
METRO BOOKS
New York

the
home color selector

METRO BOOKS
New York

An Imprint of Sterling Publishing
387 Park Avenue South
New York, NY 10016

ISBN: 978-1-4351-0651-2

For information about custom editions, special sales, and premium and corporate purchases, please contact
Sterling Special Sales at 800-805-5489 or specialsales@sterlingpublishing.com.

Manufactured in China

5 7 9 10 8 6 4

www.sterlingpublishing.com

Note: Colors identified in the index are from the Benjamin Moore Color System.
Every effort has been made to match colors as closely as possible, but owing to
printing limitations, colors may not match exactly. Always consult your
local supplier before purchase.

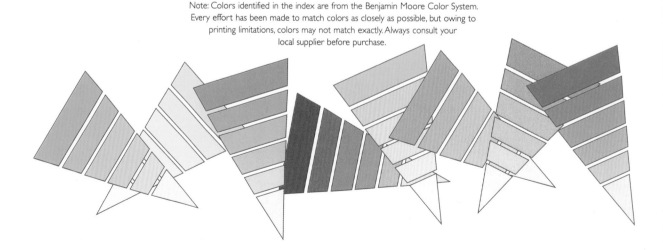

contents

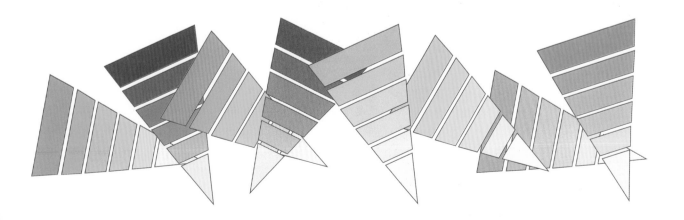

Introduction

Color creates impact and atmosphere, and is one of the first things that people notice when entering a room. Color can make a home appear bright and fresh, or grand and formal; it can change the look and feel of a home almost instantly. Color also has mood-enhancing qualities, so it is essential that we surround ourselves with colors that we like and make us feel good inside our homes.

A bold combination of two complementary colors, orange and blue, creates an invigorating space that would suit a dynamic expressive type, but could overwhelm a more reclusive individual.

It is tempting when redesigning a home to choose colors that are in fashion at the present time. We are influenced by many factors; photographs in magazines, store displays, friend's homes, and television shows, for example, and it can be difficult to focus on what we actually like and respond to. It may be that you like a wide range of colors, and find it difficult to decide. The Home Color Selector can help you to refine your choices and understand how the choices you make will change the feel of your home. It can also help you to find ways to combine colors and work out which shades harmonize, and which will contrast. If you are trying to create a particular mood in your home, such as 'tranquil', 'elegant', or 'fresh', you can turn to the relevant chapter and find the exact colors that will help you to achieve your aim.

Color schemes for lifestyles

When buying your home, you probably had an idea of the type of lifestyle you were hoping to create. A sophisticated, urban retreat to relax in at the end of the day, or a contemporary family home? An elegant county home or a fresh, light space where you can work? Choosing the right colors can help you to achieve the 'feel' you aspire to. You may have a scheme already in your head, but want to check that it will work. Sometimes we want to repeat favorite colors that we have lived with before, or we want a complete change, or we may wish to try a scheme that we have seen elsewhere. Magazines and books are great for inspiration, but you also need to think about how they will work in your home and with your lifestyle.

For example, a minimalist scheme that uses neutral, tranquil colors may be ideal for a person who leads a hectic life, and longs for calm, but if you secretly crave a relaxing cocoon, you may need warmer colors in your home. A family with young children may find a neutral color scheme hard to maintain, but may want to capture that sense of calm as much as possible.

175   4

The combination of deep red walls with the rich textures of the natural wood creates a warm cozy dining room, that has a timeless elegance.

Introduction continued

82 **815**

Alternating areas of light
and shade and the cool
color scheme of white walls
with deep blue upholstery
combine to make a very
contemporary room that is
extremely tranquil.

Strong, vibrant colors can bring energy and vitality to a home, especially in social areas, and may bring interest to a room that does not get good natural light. Strong, rich colors create an atmosphere that we respond to immediately, while the effects of softer tones take longer for us to notice. However, it can be difficult to agree on strong colors, and in a shared home, they may be best restricted to accent colors.

If you yearn for bold colors, but your partner dislikes the idea, use the Home Color Selector to find colors that harmonize together, and use the bold colors in soft furnishings or art. Bear in mind that the colors in the rooms where we spend a long time will have a more profound and lasting effect on our moods than those in areas we just pass through. For example, a bold paint color on a feature wall in the hallway may lift your spirits when you enter your home, but may be overpowering in the main sitting room. A bold color in a child's room can be fun, but it may also stop them relaxing at bedtime!

In order to relax and feel comfortable, you need

to find a color scheme that all the occupants of your home like. If a room is decorated in colors that make someone feel uncomfortable, they will instinctively avoid spending time there. This is the reason many of us walk into a new home and want to change everything! If you are constantly surrounded by colors you do not like, you will find it difficult to relax in your home. A strong color chosen by one person in the family, may irritate others, for example, few men would feel comfortable in a very pink room.

793 **382**

Light cool colors such as the blue of these kitchen cabinets in combination with the white walls and green plants help to reflect the maximum amount of light into the room, keeping it fresh and bright.

25 **337**

The deep firey orange of the color-washed walls could be overpowering, but here it is offset by the distressed timber panelling, and, with candles lit makes for a sensual bathing experience.

how to use this book

This book is divided into three sections.

Chapter one:
Talking color explains how to use the color wheel on the front of the book, along with an explanation of the basic principles of color theory. This includes how colors harmonize, together with an explanation of the key terms relating to color, such as hue, tone, and saturation.

Chapter two:
Color Personality contains an overview of how colors make us feel, and how we can use that to create the style of home we want. We introduce the moods that will be used in the Color Combinations section: tranquil, invigorating, elegant, sensual, and fresh.

Chapter three:
The Color Schemes section includes a comprehensive directory of color swatch combinations, so you can see at a glance which colors work together, and the effects combining colors will produce. The combinations are divided into moods and organised further into warm, cool, and neutral shades. Each color is from the Benjamin Moore paint range, so you can use the reference number to source the paint choice you have made.

132 HOME**COLOR**SELECTOR

| 20 | 339 |
| 175 | 21 |

RIGHT Strong contrasts such as blue and yellow work well, particularly if one is used for accents such as pillows. This scheme is kept from being overpowering by the soft warm wall, which breaks up the intensity of the stronger contrasting tones.

| 20 | 662 |
| 443 | 871 |

LEFT The combination of cream, white and yellow offset the black work surface and give this room a fresh quality and a golden glow making it a pleasant space to spend time.

| | 471 |
| 366 | 175 |

RIGHT By varying the tones of blue from light to dark and by adding touches of contrast, as in the full bowl of fruit, this cool kitchen is brought to life.

INVIGORATING**COLOR**SCHEMES 133

main colors used in room sets enable instant access to unique color references

inspirational photographs demonstrate how color schemes and moods work in real homes and settings

each page features four color schemes based around the main mood color All colors are selected from the Benjamin Moore Classic and Affinity ranges

choose the adjacent color swatch for monochrome schemes (see pages 22-23), these are easier to harmonize as all the hues are related

within elegant, tranquil, invigirating, sensual and fresh, schemes are divided by warm, neutral and cool

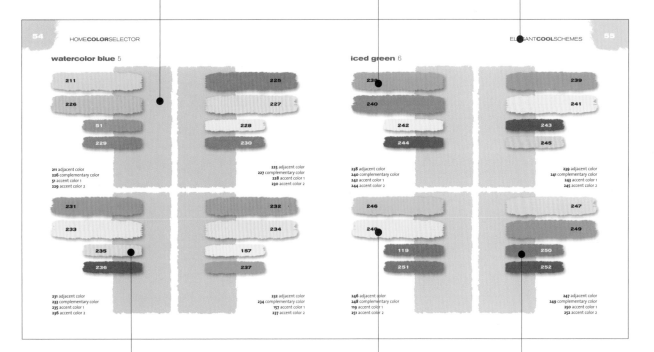

54 HOME**COLOR**SELECTOR

ELE**GANT****COOL**SCHEMES 55

watercolor blue 5

211
226
51
229

225
227
228
230

211 adjacent color
226 complementary color
51 accent color 1
229 accent color 2

225 adjacent color
227 complementary color
228 accent color 1
230 accent color 2

231
233
235
236

232
234
157
237

231 adjacent color
233 complementary color
235 accent color 1
236 accent color 2

232 adjacent color
234 complementary color
157 accent color 1
237 accent color 2

iced green 6

238
240
242
244

239
241
243
245

238 adjacent color
240 complementary color
242 accent color 1
244 accent color 2

239 adjacent color
241 complementary color
243 accent color 1
245 accent color 2

246
248
119
251

247
249
250
252

246 adjacent color
248 complementary color
119 accent color 1
251 accent color 2

247 adjacent color
249 complementary color
250 accent color 1
252 accent color 2

the color swatches are organized by adjacent color, complementary color, and two accent colors; each color has a unique reference number so you can source the colors you have selected in the index to the Benjamin Moore color range

choose the complementary color if you like schemes that add vitality and energy into a room

select either accent swatch, or even both, to select a color suggestion for accessories and soft furnishing that will contrast and enliven your scheme.

talking
color

When you walk into a room that has been designed by a professional interior designer, it usually feels 'right'. The room feels inviting, it has interest, and everything seems to work together. This is because a designer has learned how to bring color and texture together in ways that are harmonious and pleasing, without being safe or boring. Understanding some of the basic principals behind why some colors work together, and why some don't will help you make choices you are happy with, and that create a professional look. It also helps to understand terms such as hue and saturation when working with design professionals. This chapter gives a brief overview of the basic ideas behind color theory, and how you can use it to your advantage.

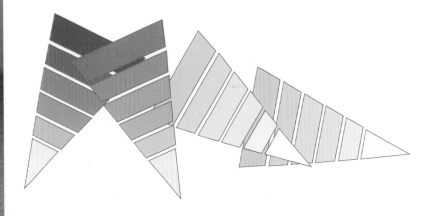

the color wheel

Before you start choosing subtle shades, it is useful to understand how color works. Working out if colors go together, whether they create harmony or contrast is made easier by understanding how colors sit together on a 'color wheel'.

A color wheel can help us to create color schemes that work. A color wheel is a visual way of showing how colors appear in the visible spectrum, as in a rainbow, from red to violet. The three primary colors are red, yellow, and blue and most of us learn how to mix these at school, creating greens, purples, and oranges from these basic colors. Shown on a color wheel, the primary colors form the spokes of the color wheel. The greens, purples, and oranges are known as secondary colors, and these are also shown on the wheel. Tertiary colors are mixtures of primary and secondary hues, and form another triangle on the color wheel; each adding more complexity and variety.

Colors that are closest to each other on the color wheel are most harmonious. The colors on the opposite side of the wheel provide the greatest contrast; these are called complementary. For example, a harmonious scheme would include shades of blue and purple, while a contrasting scheme would include blue with orange. This color wheel shows bold colors but the same principle applies to more muted shades. Complementary colors balance and excite one another. You can use them to create lively contrasts and dramatic effects, for example, for an invigorating scheme. Harmonious colors are a safer choice for an elegant or tranquil scheme.

ORANGE (SECONDARY COLOR)

Orange is a secondary color made up of red and yellow. It can be combined with its complementary color, blue, to create a warm and invigorating effect. When orange is combined with pale, neutral colors, such as cream, it creates a calm, warm, sensual effect.

YELLOW (PRIMARY COLOR)

Yellow is one of the three primary colors and works well with green shades. Imagine pale, crisp yellows and greens making a fresh, bright color scheme for a breakfast room. Yellow contrasts with purple and violet, which may look extreme in many adult rooms, but it would look fun in a child's bedroom. Pale shades of violet and yellow can work very well together, creating a lively contrast.

GREEN (SECONDARY COLOR)

Green is a versatile color. Dark, rich greens can work well in a formal, elegant room, especially when combined with harmonious blues and gold-yellows. Contrast with reds for eye-catching contrast that are perhaps best used in accessories. Pale greens are often teamed with pale yellows in wallpapers and soft furnishings, to create bright, fresh, but harmonious country schemes.

RED-ORANGE

ORANGE

ORANGE-YELLOW

YELLOW

YELLOW-GREEN

GREEN

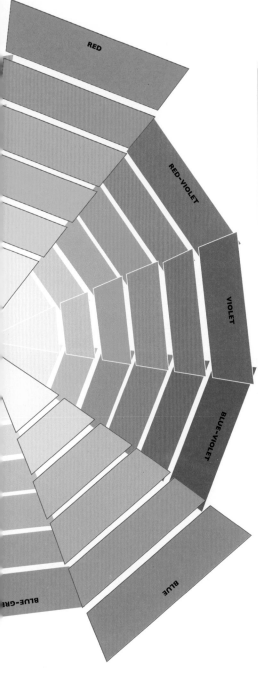

RED (PRIMARY COLOR)

The most powerful of the primary colors, red can be used to create a range of moods, from the comforting and cozy, to the dramatic and luxurious. It is harmonious with oranges and purples to create rich, sensual rooms. Using a small amount in a neutral room can add warmth and personality. Contrast red with blue or green for striking effects.

VIOLET (SECONDARY COLOR)

Purples and violets can be warm, rich, and luxurious. They are harmonious with blues and when used alongside warm neutrals, they can create very appealing room schemes. Purples contrast with oranges, which would be overpowering for many people, but used sparingly or for deliberate effect in art or soft furnishings, striking contrasts can add real impact to a room.

BLUE (PRIMARY COLOR)

A versatile color, blue can work well with its immediate neighbor, violet, both in pale pastel shades, and rich sensual shades. Blue and green are neighbors in nature, and also harmonize in many color schemes. Be aware that you need to choose shades from the same Color Personality section for harmony; a dark shade of blue would dominate a pale green, and vice versa.

HOW TO USE THE COLOR WHEEL

The color wheel on the cover of the book shows you some of the main colors from each color personality: tranquil, invigorating, elegant, sensual, and fresh. For example, if you want a blue scheme, you can turn the wheel to see which shades of blue will create each personality. If you want a bright, lively blue for a sunny kitchen room, turn the wheel to 'fresh' to find a shade that will best suit your scheme. For an elegant evening room, turn the wheel to 'elegant' to find a sophisticated shade. The wheel offers a small selection of shades to help you start your search; turn to the relevant chapters for more shades and combinations.

COMPLEMENTARY COLORS

HARMONIOUS COLORS

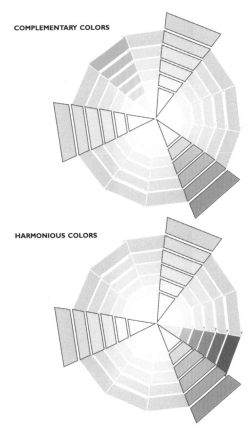

hues and saturation

Hue is another word for color. The colors on the spectrum color wheel are 'pure', saturated hues. The color is at its purest and most intense. Saturation refers to the purity of a hue. When fully saturated, a hue is at its most intense.

We rarely choose colors for our homes that are strong and saturated, finding them too bold and rich. Most of us prefer more subtle, muted tones. Colors become less saturated when whites, creams, and grays are added. When we add white to pure hues they become lighter; this is known as a 'tint'. Tint shades appear more alive and reflect more light than spectrum colors, and are often used to cre-

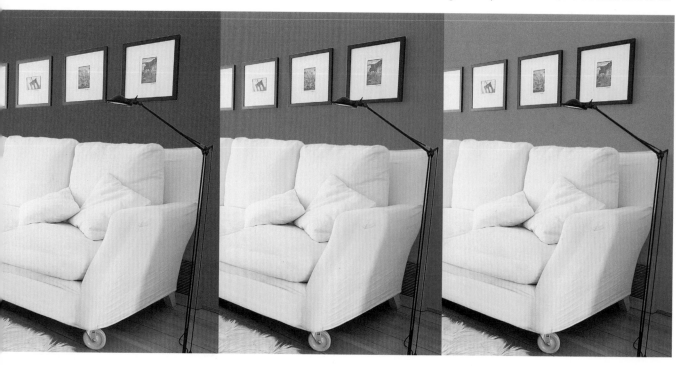

This is an example of using a fully saturated color, deep orange, to produce a rich effect, ideal for formal social events. Saturated hues can be combined with their complementary colors, such as orange with blue, to create a vibrant color scheme.

Here, a little white has been added to lighten the orange and create a warm, summery, and welcoming atmosphere, ideal for more informal social gatherings. The cream upholstery helps ensure that the overall effect is not too stimulating.

In this picture, much more white has been added to the orange to create a tint. By lightening the color of the background to this degree, the room now seems much more open and airy, suitable to be the main family room, and for general activities.

ate fresh and invigorating schemes, as they help to bring light in to a space. Tints are often called pastels or powder colors; pink is a tint of red, while peach is a tint of orange. Tints are easy to live with. To create a harmonious scheme, you could use various tints from one color group. To create a contrasting scheme, choose tints from opposite sides of a color wheel. A 'shade' is a hue to which black has been added, making it appear darker than the spectrum color from which it is derived. This can make a dramatic change. For example, adding black to red will turn it into maroon, while a shade of yellow will become brown. Decorating with a range of shades derived from the same color group can create an elegant, harmonious scheme, for example, creams with shades of chocolate brown.

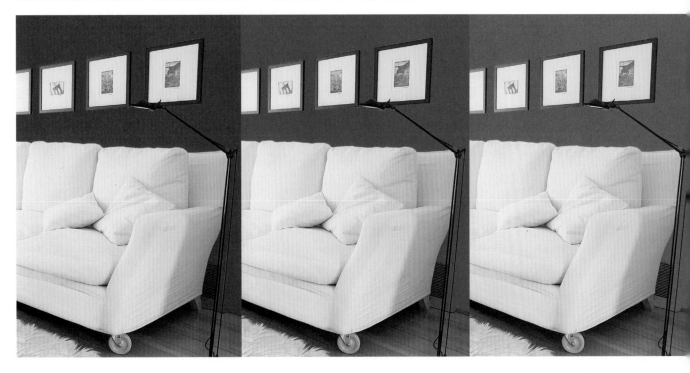

Deep saturation allows the hue's natural intensity and qualities to be used to maximum effect. Here, the deep indigo of the walls creates a cocooned space that feels warming, intimate, and secure—a haven on cold winter evenings.

Gray and white has been added to the pure hue to create a cooler, more subtle tone that is less vibrant and imposing. The room now seems more elegant, a suitable venue for activities such as light reading or study.

The more gray you add, the more muted and neutral the color becomes, creating a more subtle and less distinctive mood. The room appears both relaxing and inspiring, a place to recharge the batteries while planning the day ahead.

hues and tones

We talk about 'tone' when talking about the lightness or darkness of one hue compared with another. A tone is light or dark depending on whether black, white, or gray has been added. The tone of a color can also indicate its brilliance and luminosity.

Tones are more muted and dusky colors, and they are less bright than the spectrum colors. A tone can be either light or dark depending on whether black has been added to a light color or white to a dark color. Tones are popular in decorating schemes, as the effect is matt and sophisticated, and creates a sophisticated, elegant look. They are ideal for social rooms such as sitting rooms, or dining rooms, and several tones of one color can be used together to create a harmonious scheme. Choosing the right tone for your room is therefore as important as selecting the right hue. For example, if you want a blue room, but one that is 'elegant' rather than 'invigorating', choose one of the blue tones from pages 40-57. A blue from another section would look too bright and jarring.

We tend to think of a color as just one tone, whereas a single color can often reflect more than one wavelength of light, giving it an iridescent quality like that of a peacock's feather or mother-of-pearl shell. The color showing through is known as an undertone.

These photographs show how different tones of yellow can create different schemes, from fresh to elegant.

RIGHT A pale tone of yellow creates a spacious and airy feel, ideal for a 'fresh' scheme.

FAR RIGHT This yellow is slightly darker than the first but still has good saturation that creates an 'invigorating' look.

Dark, fully saturated tones have the most brilliance and intensity and so make the most impact. Use to create 'elegant', rich schemes.

color temperature

When trying to achieve a certain feel in a room, think about whether you need a 'hot' or 'cold' temperature color. A room that does not get much natural light may need a 'warm' color to add warmth and richness. Reds and oranges tend to have a warming effect, and blues tend to have a cooling effect on a room.

Generally, reds and oranges (the colors of fire) are warm, and blues and greens (the colors of sea, sky, and plants) are cool, with other colors on the wheel falling in between. However, it is not always that simple! Some blues are warmer than others, and some reds cooler than others. If a blue has a great deal of gray or white in it, it can look very cold. This would be a poor choice for a dark bathroom, which could look cold and uninviting. However, a blue that contains a lot of yellow can look warm and inviting. Similarly, a red that contains a lot of blue can appear cold; this can be a sophisticated color for an elegant scheme, but may be cold and uninviting in a dark day room.

The temperature of a color is affected by its undertone and whether a hue has a warm or cool look. Every color can be regarded as either hot or cold depending on its undertone. So, for example, even though we think of red as being a hot color, it may well have a cool undertone. When you look through the Color Personality sections, you will see that there are 'cool' colors in the fresh section, and 'warm' colors in the elegant and sensual sections; although you may be looking for yellows, for example, each has its own distinct color temperature which can influence the final effect of your scheme.

This photograph enables you to see the effect of color temperature on a room. Generally, blue is the coolest color, relaxing and calming, and useful in quiet areas of the home. Greens are also cool. Yellow is bright and cheerful, ideal for a sunny kitchen, for example. Orange and red are the warmest colors. Orange is cheery, while red is stimulating. You can make use of these qualities in your decorating schemes.

WARM AND COOL COLOR SCHEMES

When the walls of the room are a warm yellow, the effect is fresh yet inviting. If you have good natural light, this color would look bright. With poor natural light, this color would look darker and more formal. The same room shown in black and white.

When the walls of the room are a cool blue, the room looks colder, although still fresh. If your room had poor natural light, this blue may appear too cold. Although the rooms are different in feel and look, it is clear from comparing black-and-white photographs that the blue is similar to the yellow in terms of color value.

color harmonies and contrasts

Choosing colors that work well together is not always easy. For example, if you are cautious and choose whites and creams only, your scheme can look boring, cold and unwelcoming. However, adding stark contrasting colors can make a room feel uncoordinated and cluttered. Successful color schemes use harmonious colors, with subtle contrast accent colors.

Knowing which colors work well together comes from trying colors alongside each other and really looking at the effect they create. Some people really know how to put colors together but it is always useful to check on the color wheel to see if you are right. The overall aim is to find the right balance so that the colors you use look harmonious and pleasing. Harmonious colors appear next to each other on the color wheel (see page 14), or use shades and tones of the same hue (see page 16). Choosing harmonious colors are essential if you are trying to create a sensual or relaxing scheme. You may want to introduce contrasting colors to liven up a fresh or invigorating scheme, but you can still aim for harmony.

MONOCHROME HARMONY

A color scheme based on one color (monochrome) is an easy way to achieve harmony. Choose different shades and tones of a single color. You could choose the main color of your existing furniture and base your scheme on that. Turn to the Color Personality section that you want to achieve and vary the tones from very light to dark. In this picture, various shades of blue and white create a harmonious, interesting space. A dark shade has been used on the wall, and lighter colors have been used in the bed linen.

CONTRAST HARMONY

This form of harmony instils vitality and life into a basic color scheme by introducing touches of strong contrasting colors. Here for example, two contrasting accent colors, the red of the flowers and the blue-green of the vase, have been introduced into a monochromatic scheme so that they bring a much-needed excitement into an otherwise neutral, calm environment.

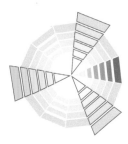

COMPLEMENTARY HARMONY

The purple and yellow work very well together, although from opposite sides of the color wheel. Subtle shades of the yellow and purple mean that this scheme is harmonious. Bright tones of purple and yellow would be too harsh and bright to live with in a bedroom. This effective scheme is elegant and sensual.

DECIDING ON A COLOR

One way of deciding whether colors are right for you is to consider carefully what your expectations are for your home. When choosing colors to suit your lifestyle, remember that the rules of color harmony still apply. For example, if you envisage your home as:

- a peaceful retreat: use soft tones, with greens, blues, and violets.

- a party house: use hot, bright, dramatic colors.

- a creative haven: use a mix of your favorite colors to stimulate the brain, or go cool and harmonious for a peaceful space.

- a place to relax: use neutral and light tones that harmonize.

- a busy family home: use warm hues for living areas and cool colors for private spaces.

- a sensual, exotic space: use a combination of deep, rich colors, ideal for night time.

- an aesthetic masterpiece: use muted tones and a restricted palette.

ADJACENT HARMONY

This scheme uses colors that are next to each other on the color wheel. The blue-grays and the greens belong to the same family of colors, and naturally look good next to each other in a color scheme. The wooden cabinets would work well in most schemes. The silver of the range and hood adds light to the space and brings harmony to the scheme.

color
personality

The colors we use in our homes reflect our personalities, but they also have personalities of their own. These are based on their own qualities, but also on our personal associations. Associations may vary among cultures, but all colors trigger a personal, emotional response, based on memory and past experience. Colors remembered from childhood homes, for example, can evoke feelings of contentment that you may want to bring to your home, whether you know it or not.

The personality of a color can be a guide to where to use it in your home, as different colors can alter the way you respond to and use a room. Each section in this chapter will show you which colors will create a specific personality in a room. For example, if you want to create an elegant room, turn to the section on Elegant Colors (see pages 40-57) to find the colors that evoke that feeling. This is also useful if you are looking for a particular shade, and want to know what effect it will create. For example, if you are drawn to certain shades of blue, you may discover that you like fresh or invigorating shades, rather than warm sensual ones.

using color to change a room

The colors we choose for our home offer an important means of self-expression. They tell us who we are and reflect our attitudes, lifestyle, and what image we want to portray to the outside world. They also create a feeling in a home that anyone will pick up as soon as they enter.

A color's personality can transform a room. When choosing a room color, you need to take into account your personality and style preference, but you also need to consider the feeling you want to evoke and how you plan to use the room.

The personality of a color can be a guide to where to use it in your home, as different colors can alter the way you respond and use a room. If you want to feel more sociable, you might introduce red tones. If you prefer a quieter life, include some calming blue or green.

You may also choose colors because you want to create or convey a particular style or design idea. If you want to achieve a neutral, sophisticated look, turn to

PERSONALITY CHECKLIST

Outlines of the personalities of the main color groups are given below. As you select colors in the book, you may like to refer back to this list to see what your choices say about you, and what affect the colors will have in your home. Like everything in life, an excess can change a positive into negative, so it is wise not to use too much of any one color in your home.

RED
STRONG, VIBRANT
It is the color of blood, fire, and passion. At the same time, this eye-catching color is also the color of love and happiness. Red is warm, energetic, and vibrant. People who like red are dynamic and sociable. It would be a good choice for creating an invigorating or sensual space. Use red in family rooms or formal dining rooms, where activity counts over relaxation.

ORANGE
CREATIVE, FUN-LOVING
It is a striking color that we associate with the sun, ripe peaches, late-summer flowers, so orange has strong sensual connections and a built-in feel-good factor. Orange is as exciting as red, but less bold; it is ideal for brightening dull spaces. The orange personality is happy and favors companionship. Even lighter tones of orange are stimulating.

YELLOW
BRIGHT, ALERT
In daylight we feel safe, alert, and active, and so we think of yellow as a warm, friendly color. Yet we see green-yellow as decay in nature and so associate negative emotions with these hues. Yellow is bright and warming, and makes us feel optimistic, which is ideal for a room you use in the morning. A yellow household suggests a happy, healthy lifestyle, where the inhabitants are cheerful and full of ideas.

GREEN
HARMONIOUS, RESTFUL
Spring greens are linked to growth and youthfulness, and create a light, airy mood in a room, while darker greens are more lush and mysterious and make a much bolder statement. Soothing, fresh, and clean, green is the color of nature and growth, and is very relaxing. Dark, rich greens can be more formal, with elegant characteristics.

the elegant section (see pages 40-57) or the tranquil section (see pages 88-105). To create a warm, welcoming space, for example, in a family room, look at the section on invigorating colors (see pages 112-129).

Consider also the function of the room. You may want your sitting room to be a sophisticated, tranquil space, ideal for evening entertaining. A bedroom will feel more relaxing if you choose colors for their sensual properties, rather than colors with stimulating properties. Yet you may need these spaces to link together, without clashing.

You may be choosing colors because you want to market your property and create a 'lifestyle' that will appeal to specific buyers. An urban luxury apartment may suit elegant or tranquil colors, for example, and a tired property in need of updating may benefit from adding invigorating or fresh colors.

Before selecting your choice, remember to consider the size of the room and the amount of light it gets. A room that gets very little natural light may need fresh colors, or you may decide to go with the natural features, and make it a subdued, sensual room.

PINK

SECURITY AND TRUST
We are drawn to pink when we need reassurance. Loving and nurturing, the pink personality expresses the romantic nature of love so may be suitable for a bedroom. The inhabitants of a pink household are likely to be caring and compassionate to others.

PURPLE

DEEP, INTENSE, EMOTIONAL, EXOTIC
Purple stimulates the mind as well as the senses. People who favor purple like luxury and drama. People who live in purple homes are individuals. Time with them is unlikely to be forgotten. Purple can bring sensuality to a home.

NEUTRALS

FLEXIBLE AND RELAXING
Lovers of neutral shades value independence, and do not want to be pigeonholed. Tones of beige, gray, cream, and off-white are always popular and can provide a background to bolder color in soft furnishings and art. They can also be used alone to create a subtle, relaxing atmosphere.

VIOLET

DRAMATIC, MYSTERIOUS
This is reflected in the symbolism of this color in many religions and is reinforced by its appearance in nature. Sparkling minerals such as amethysts, and the patterns found in the iridescent plumage of some birds and on the wings of butterflies, make violet a color of surprise and wonder. It can be used to invigorate and freshen a room or add sensuality, depending on the tone.

BLUE

QUIET, SOOTHING
Dark blues have deeper and more mysterious associations, for example with the sky at midnight. It has a strong connection with sleep and dreaming, and can be ideal for creating an elegant evening room or a relaxing bedroom. Lighter blues can be calming and ideal for creating a tranquil space.

BLACK AND WHITE

SIMPLICITY AND PURITY
Shape and texture become more important in the absence of color. Black, white, and gray can be dramatic, but can be too severe to live with without using touches of accent colors. They can create an elegant, invigorating look.

tranquil colors

SPLENDOR

SANANNAH CLAY

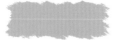

MEADOW PINK

NORTH CASCADES

WISPY GREEN

VIOLET MIST

To create a calm, peaceful, and tranquil space in your home, select colors in the Tranquil section. You can change the look and feel of a room by adding some cool, light colors. Light blues, greens, and neutrals are good choices. Faded tones are calming, but you can also introduce stronger accent colors to add warmth and comfort to a space. Pastel shades of strong colors such as orange and purple can work (see pages 88-105), but choose the tones carefully.

Be careful when choosing colors with blue tones; they can feel cold. Test the color in your room throughout the day and see what effect light falling on the color has, and whether this creates the tranquil effect you are aiming for.

Shades of white on their own can be stark rather than tranquil. Think about choosing a harmonious or complementary color, perhaps for a feature wall, or in the soft furnishings. Try several shades of white, and experiment with paint finishes; matt and eggshell paints have a softer finish than many emulsions.

Light neutrals help to maintain a feeling of space, and dark neutrals can be used to enlarge the appearance of a room by increasing its depth. Contrasting dark and light neutrals uses areas of shadow to create a room that is natural and tranquil

The natural coolness of a blue and white color scheme might not be an obvious choice for a bedroom, but contrasting it with the warm tones of the wooden bed has created a room that is a perfect place to seek tranquility.

invigorating colors

MOROCCAN SPICE

SUNRAYS

NOVA SCOTIA BLUE

WARM APPLE CRISP

LEMON GRASS

CHIC LIME

To create a lively, invigorating space use rich, warm hues. Using bright, hot harmonies will bring energy and vitality to your home; ideal for a breakfast room or bathroom. Warm reds, oranges, and yellows can bring richness and sunshine to a room. Very dark reds and oranges, however, can create a formal feel, so select the right tone for your light conditions.

Bright tones of most colors can create invigorating effects; lime greens, turquoise blues, and zesty lemons stimulate the mind and bring energy to a space. If a room has good natural light, these colors will enliven any room. Be careful that dark light conditions will dull these colors, and can create a murky effect.

If you are nervous of introducing large areas of an invigorating color, consider using it as an accent. Artwork, cushions, or a floorcovering can introduce an invigorating color into a room, without overpowering.

TOP RIGHT Changing the color of, or adding cushions to a room is an easy and quick way of introducing strong color.

RIGHT The flowing curve of the mosaics, and the strong contrast between red and blue bring an invigorating atmosphere to an otherwise neutral bathroom.

Yellow is a warm color without the heat of red or orange. Rather than stimulating the body, yellow energizes the mind, and when exposed to it, it can have a beneficial effect on our analytical capabilities.

elegant colors

BOTTLE OF BORDEAUX

PRINCESS

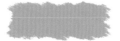

BALTIC GRAY

MAPLE SYRUP

WATERCOLOR BLUE

ICED GREEN

When we think of elegance, we think of formal rooms, styled to make an impression. Elegant colors could be used in an entrance hall, a sitting room, or a dining room. Neutrals are ideal for creating elegant spaces; they are calm and sophisticated, and act as a backdrop to display items. Tones can be warm or cool, depending on the look you want to achieve. Taupes, whites, creams, and grays can evoke elegance, especially when teamed with textures in soft furnishings. Soft metallic colors can be elegant, if used as an occasional accent and can add warmth and glamour.

When thinking of elegance, also consider rich, luxurious colors, such as purples, reds, greens, and blues. Historically associated with wealth, rich color hues can add understated drama and opulence. Use sparingly as an accent to add warmth, especially to a formal evening room. Select tones that harmonize with your main neutral color to avoid garish clashing combinations.

The blue-gray kitchen cabinets against the soft cream of the walls provide a perfect setting for the rich plum island centerpiece, creating an elegant and timeless style.

Decorating your bathroom in colors that suggest water, can really improve the way you use it. Using cool colors such as blues and greens make a bathroom look fresh, clean, and elegant, and can act as a reminder of revitalizing places by the sea, lakes, or rivers, that help create a positive frame of mind.

sensual colors

ULTRA VIOLET

BURNT SIENNA

PARIS ROMANCE

TUCSON TAN

FREESIA

SECRET

To create an intimate space, perhaps in a bedroom or formal sitting room, sensual colors can be used to great effect. This group has two personalities; muted, soft and luxurious colors, and stimulating, rich colors. Select muted, warm creams, whites, and browns to provide a soft background to a scheme, and to suggest luxury and comfort. The sensual neutrals are subdued and subtle; nothing should be too bold or jarring; no bright whites or stark contrasts. Choose colors that are close in tone, and are adjacent on the color wheel to create harmony.

The second group are stimulating and rich, such as deep reds, burgundys, purples, and chocolate browns. Associated with passion and sensuality, these sensual colors evoke drama and excitement. Use sparingly to maintain subtlety; choose one bold color for a feature wall, or introduce to a neutral scheme with throws, cushions, and light fittings.

RIGHT Using a purple will add a rich luxurious feel to a room, and when used with its complementaries, orange and yellow, it creates a warm and sensual space.

OPPOSITE The deep rich burgundy of the wall is enriched with the reflected light from the wood floor making for a dramatic entrance hall.

fresh colors

BUTTERED YAM

SAILOR'S DELIGHT

OLD STRAW HAT

HUSHED HUE

CRISP MORNING AIR

MINT JULEP

RIGHT The subtle orange tones in this breakfast room are ideal for stimulating the mind and gently invigorating the body for the start of a fresh day.

OPPOSITE Sky blue walls and natural wood are complemented perfectly by the foliage of the trees through the window, encapsulating all that is good on a fresh spring morning.

Bright, cheerful, and inspirational, fresh colors are ideal for family spaces, bathrooms, children's bedrooms, and morning rooms. Use to emphasize natural sunlight, or to inject brightness when a room lacks good natural daylight. Yellows, aquas, pale blues, and mint greens remind us of being outdoors, and being near the sea, and help to make a space feel fresh and bright.

For bathrooms, fresh blues and aquas are ideal colors, especially when teamed with bright whites.

Clean and invigorating, these shades remind us of fresh water. Choose cool tones, rather than warm for freshness, especially in a sunny room. Be careful in darker rooms as these shades can appear cold. Bright and pale yellows are ideal for introducing freshness; choose a shade according to the light conditions in your room. Avoid mustard yellows. Bright, reflective whites can make any space feel fresh; avoid white with high gray content, as this can appear gloomy.

the color
combinations

The schemes in this chapter are created using a selection of colors from the Benjamin Moore Classic and Affinity ranges. Having decided on your scheme turn to the Index on pages 156-160 to identify the unique BM number, this is all you need to take to the store and purchase your paint.

bottle of bordeaux 1

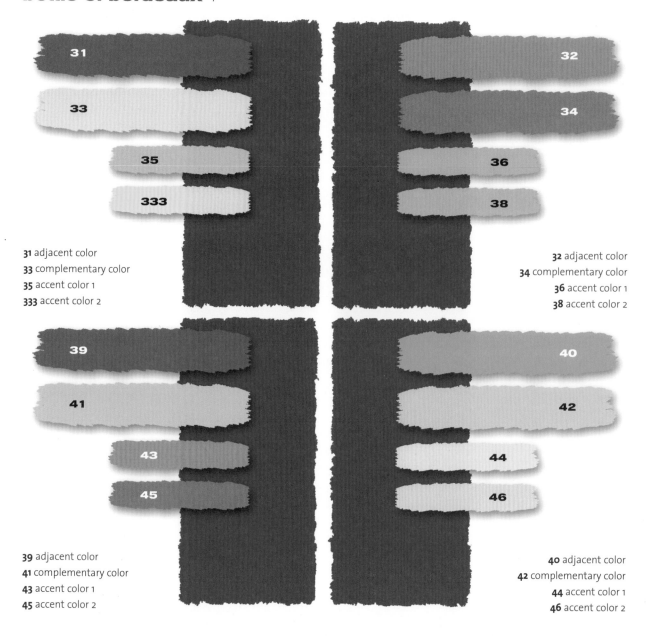

31 adjacent color
33 complementary color
35 accent color 1
333 accent color 2

32 adjacent color
34 complementary color
36 accent color 1
38 accent color 2

39 adjacent color
41 complementary color
43 accent color 1
45 accent color 2

40 adjacent color
42 complementary color
44 accent color 1
46 accent color 2

bottle of bordeaux 1

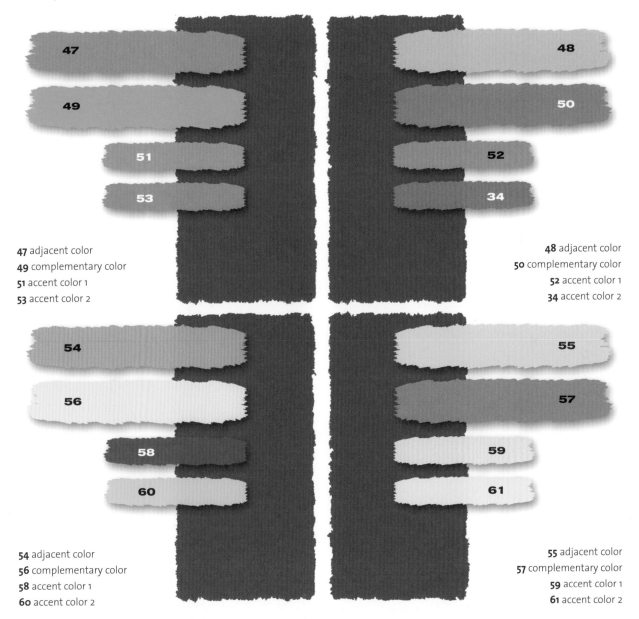

47 adjacent color
49 complementary color
51 accent color 1
53 accent color 2

48 adjacent color
50 complementary color
52 accent color 1
34 accent color 2

54 adjacent color
56 complementary color
58 accent color 1
60 accent color 2

55 adjacent color
57 complementary color
59 accent color 1
61 accent color 2

bottle of bordeaux 1

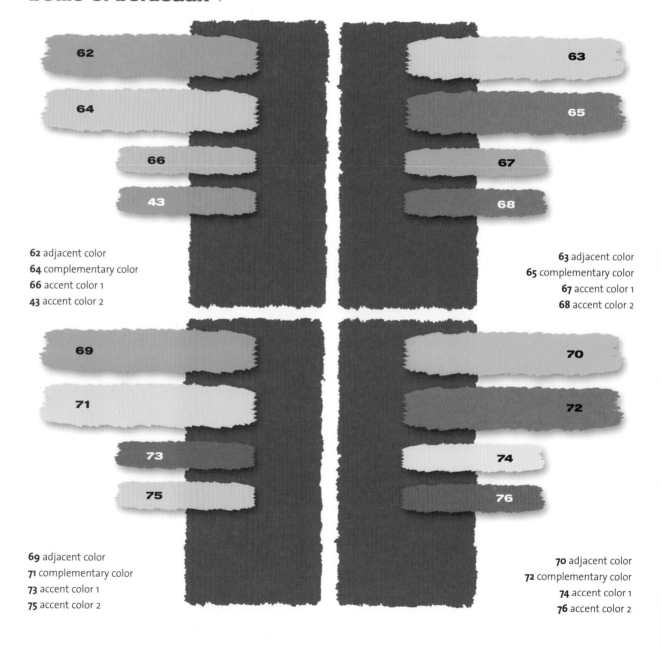

62 adjacent color
64 complementary color
66 accent color 1
43 accent color 2

63 adjacent color
65 complementary color
67 accent color 1
68 accent color 2

69 adjacent color
71 complementary color
73 accent color 1
75 accent color 2

70 adjacent color
72 complementary color
74 accent color 1
76 accent color 2

princess 2

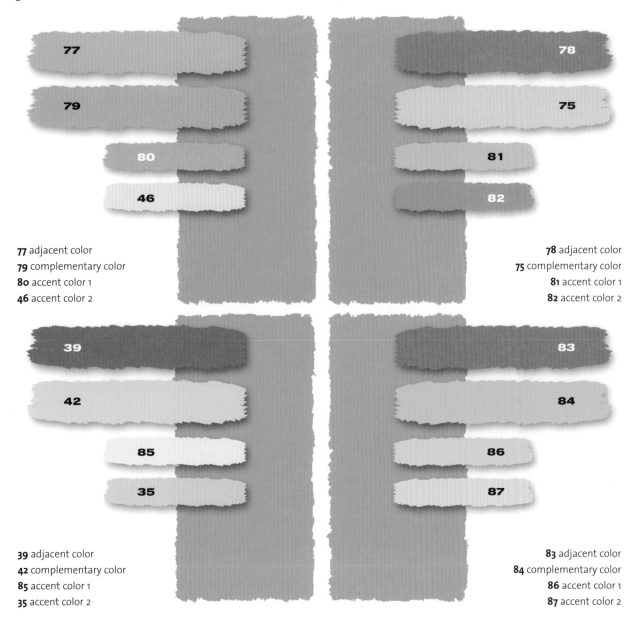

77 adjacent color
79 complementary color
80 accent color 1
46 accent color 2

78 adjacent color
75 complementary color
81 accent color 1
82 accent color 2

39 adjacent color
42 complementary color
85 accent color 1
35 accent color 2

83 adjacent color
84 complementary color
86 accent color 1
87 accent color 2

princess 2

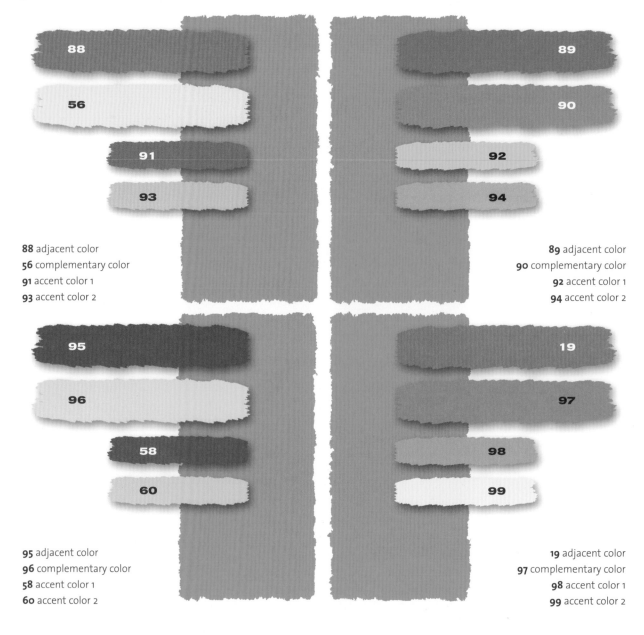

88 adjacent color
56 complementary color
91 accent color 1
93 accent color 2

89 adjacent color
90 complementary color
92 accent color 1
94 accent color 2

95 adjacent color
96 complementary color
58 accent color 1
60 accent color 2

19 adjacent color
97 complementary color
98 accent color 1
99 accent color 2

princess 2

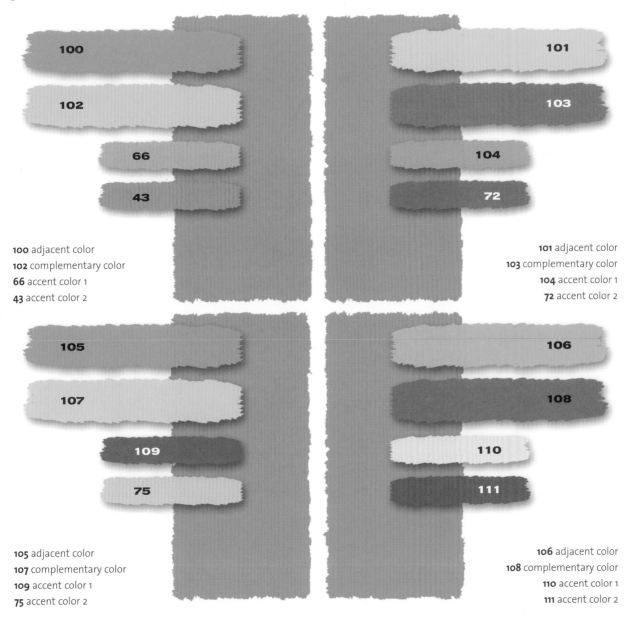

100 adjacent color
102 complementary color
66 accent color 1
43 accent color 2

101 adjacent color
103 complementary color
104 accent color 1
72 accent color 2

105 adjacent color
107 complementary color
109 accent color 1
75 accent color 2

106 adjacent color
108 complementary color
110 accent color 1
111 accent color 2

baltic gray 3

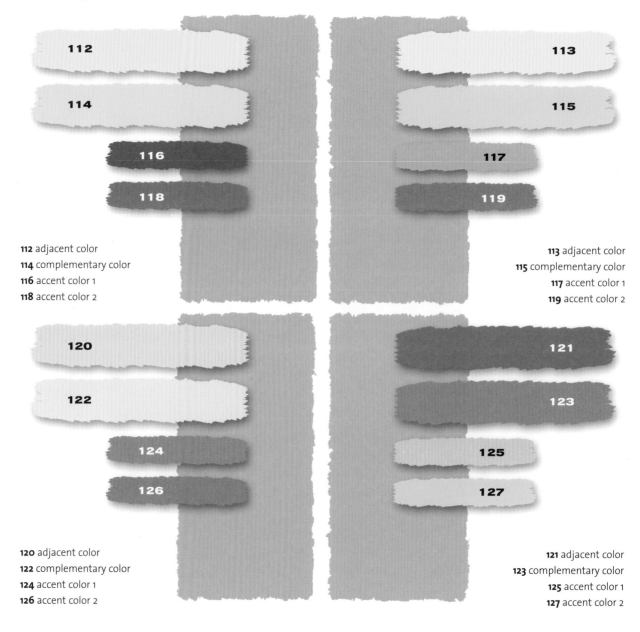

112 adjacent color
114 complementary color
116 accent color 1
118 accent color 2

113 adjacent color
115 complementary color
117 accent color 1
119 accent color 2

120 adjacent color
122 complementary color
124 accent color 1
126 accent color 2

121 adjacent color
123 complementary color
125 accent color 1
127 accent color 2

baltic gray 3

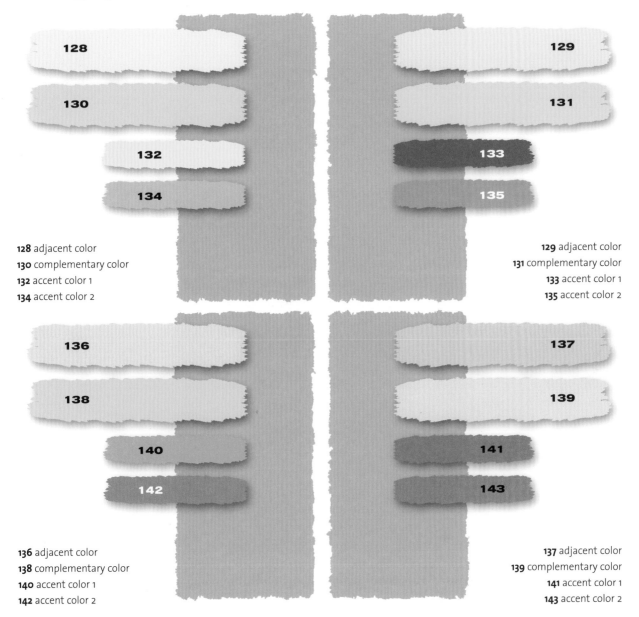

128 adjacent color
130 complementary color
132 accent color 1
134 accent color 2

129 adjacent color
131 complementary color
133 accent color 1
135 accent color 2

136 adjacent color
138 complementary color
140 accent color 1
142 accent color 2

137 adjacent color
139 complementary color
141 accent color 1
143 accent color 2

baltic gray 3

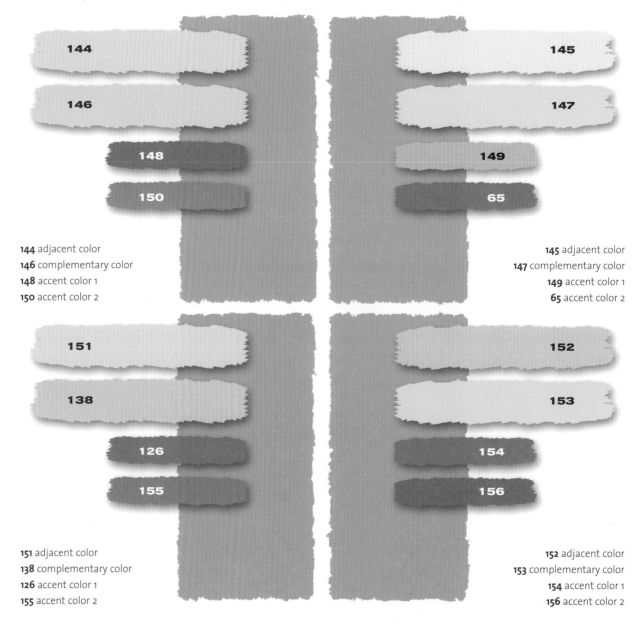

144 adjacent color
146 complementary color
148 accent color 1
150 accent color 2

145 adjacent color
147 complementary color
149 accent color 1
65 accent color 2

151 adjacent color
138 complementary color
126 accent color 1
155 accent color 2

152 adjacent color
153 complementary color
154 accent color 1
156 accent color 2

maple syrup 4

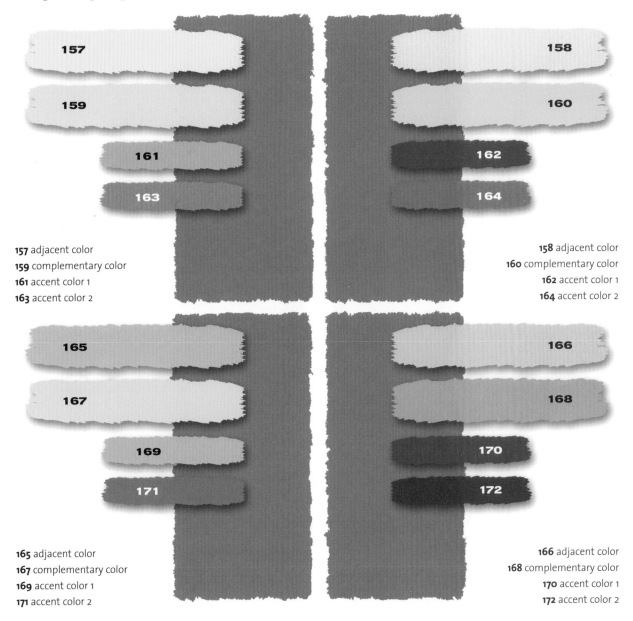

157 adjacent color
159 complementary color
161 accent color 1
163 accent color 2

158 adjacent color
160 complementary color
162 accent color 1
164 accent color 2

165 adjacent color
167 complementary color
169 accent color 1
171 accent color 2

166 adjacent color
168 complementary color
170 accent color 1
172 accent color 2

maple syrup 4

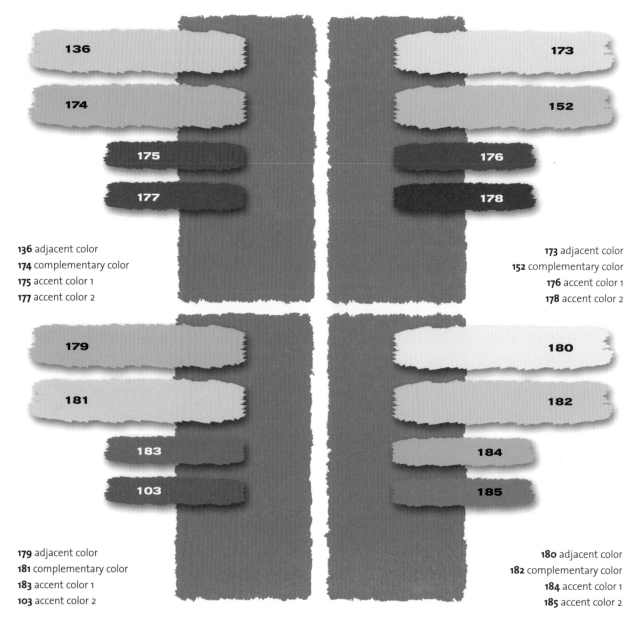

136 | 173

174 | 152

175 | 176

177 | 178

136 adjacent color
174 complementary color
175 accent color 1
177 accent color 2

173 adjacent color
152 complementary color
176 accent color 1
178 accent color 2

179 | 180

181 | 182

183 | 184

103 | 185

179 adjacent color
181 complementary color
183 accent color 1
103 accent color 2

180 adjacent color
182 complementary color
184 accent color 1
185 accent color 2

maple syrup 4

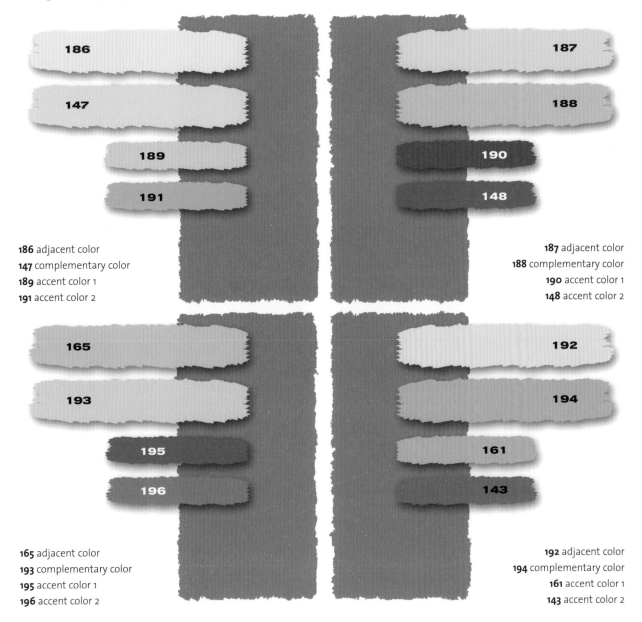

186 adjacent color
147 complementary color
189 accent color 1
191 accent color 2

187 adjacent color
188 complementary color
190 accent color 1
148 accent color 2

165 adjacent color
193 complementary color
195 accent color 1
196 accent color 2

192 adjacent color
194 complementary color
161 accent color 1
143 accent color 2

watercolor blue 5

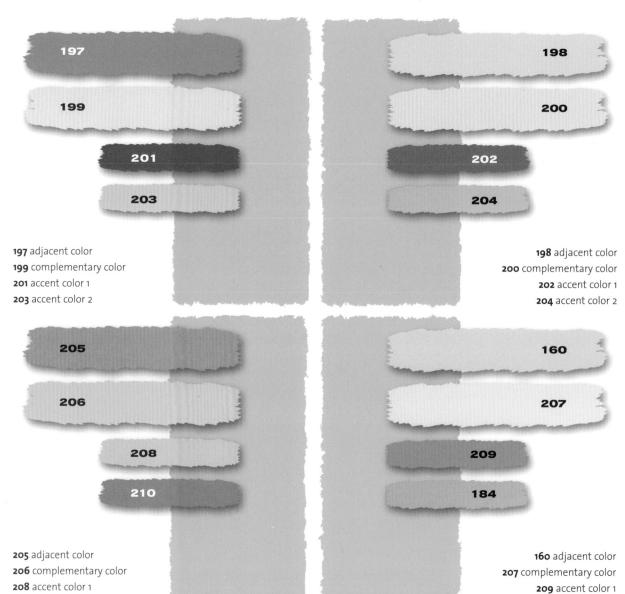

197 adjacent color
199 complementary color
201 accent color 1
203 accent color 2

198 adjacent color
200 complementary color
202 accent color 1
204 accent color 2

205 adjacent color
206 complementary color
208 accent color 1
210 accent color 2

160 adjacent color
207 complementary color
209 accent color 1
184 accent color 2

watercolor blue 5

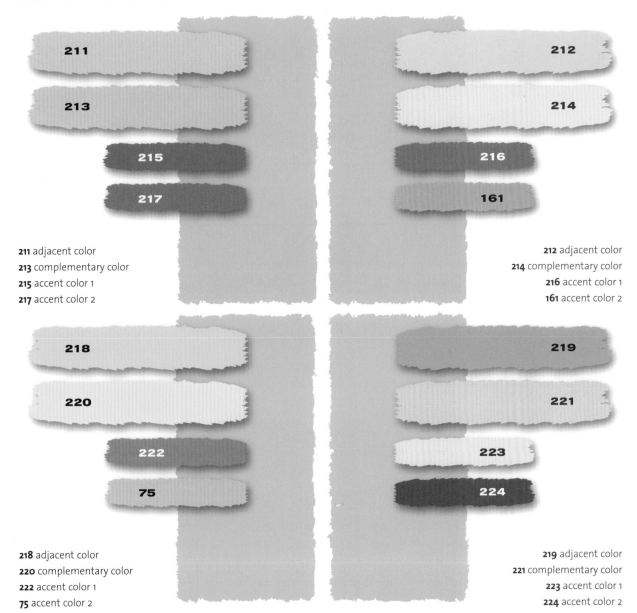

211 adjacent color
213 complementary color
215 accent color 1
217 accent color 2

212 adjacent color
214 complementary color
216 accent color 1
161 accent color 2

218 adjacent color
220 complementary color
222 accent color 1
75 accent color 2

219 adjacent color
221 complementary color
223 accent color 1
224 accent color 2

watercolor blue 5

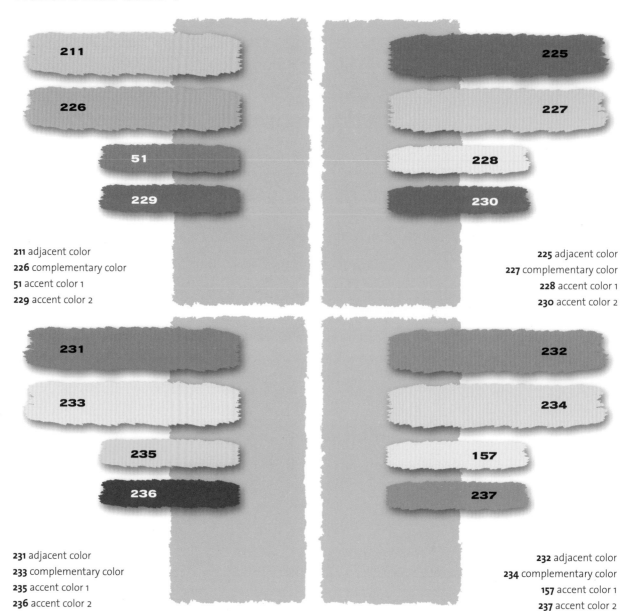

211 adjacent color
226 complementary color
51 accent color 1
229 accent color 2

225 adjacent color
227 complementary color
228 accent color 1
230 accent color 2

231 adjacent color
233 complementary color
235 accent color 1
236 accent color 2

232 adjacent color
234 complementary color
157 accent color 1
237 accent color 2

iced green 6

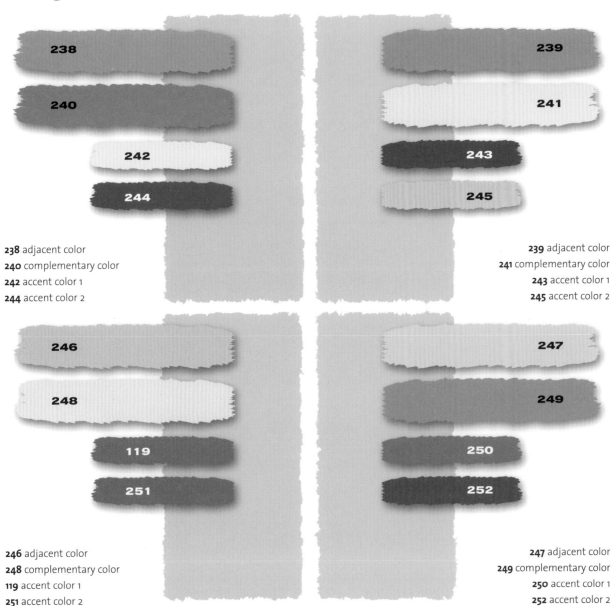

238 adjacent color
240 complementary color
242 accent color 1
244 accent color 2

239 adjacent color
241 complementary color
243 accent color 1
245 accent color 2

246 adjacent color
248 complementary color
119 accent color 1
251 accent color 2

247 adjacent color
249 complementary color
250 accent color 1
252 accent color 2

iced green 6

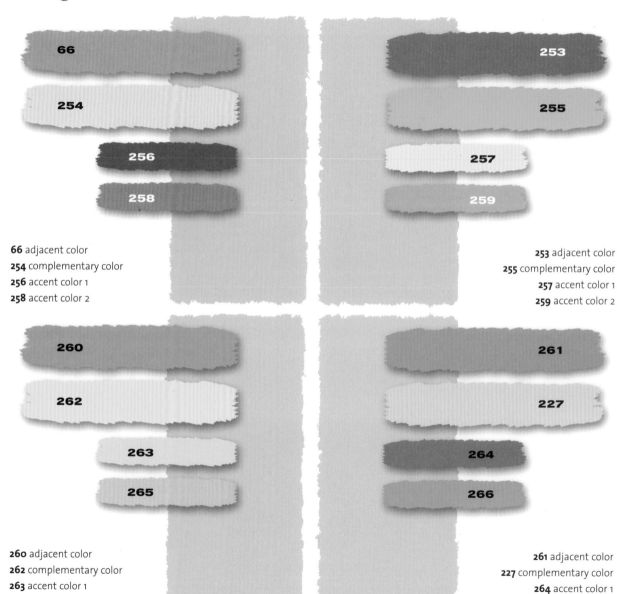

66

254

256

258

253

255

257

259

260

262

263

265

261

227

264

266

66 adjacent color
254 complementary color
256 accent color 1
258 accent color 2

253 adjacent color
255 complementary color
257 accent color 1
259 accent color 2

260 adjacent color
262 complementary color
263 accent color 1
265 accent color 2

261 adjacent color
227 complementary color
264 accent color 1
266 accent color 2

iced green 6

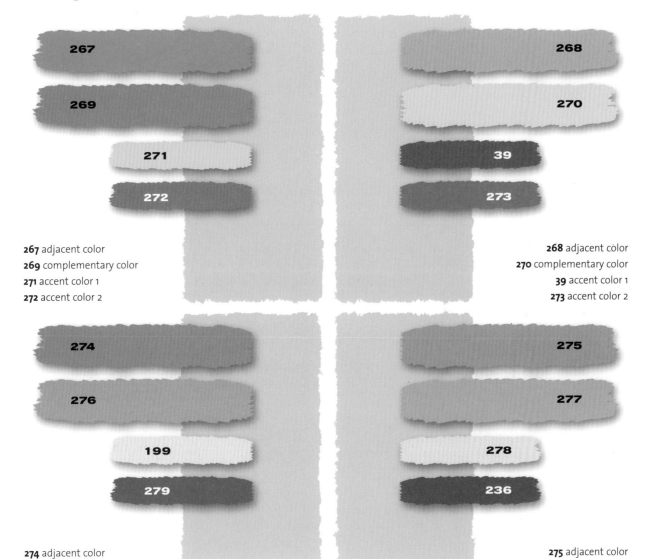

267 adjacent color
269 complementary color
271 accent color 1
272 accent color 2

268 adjacent color
270 complementary color
39 accent color 1
273 accent color 2

274 adjacent color
276 complementary color
199 accent color 1
279 accent color 2

275 adjacent color
277 complementary color
278 accent color 1
236 accent color 2

673	276
279	199

793	197
201	203

ABOVE Here the color scheme is defined by soft furnishings, the combination of these subtle shades of gray, blue, pink and brown creates a space that is elegant, cool and extremely relaxing.

RIGHT These two contrasting blues are a perfect and time-lasting color scheme for a simple classic bathroom. Here the scheme is further enhanced by the contrasting oranges and yellows of the fruit. Alternatively these contrasting colors could be introduced by means of bath towels, or decorative bottles of colored bath oils.

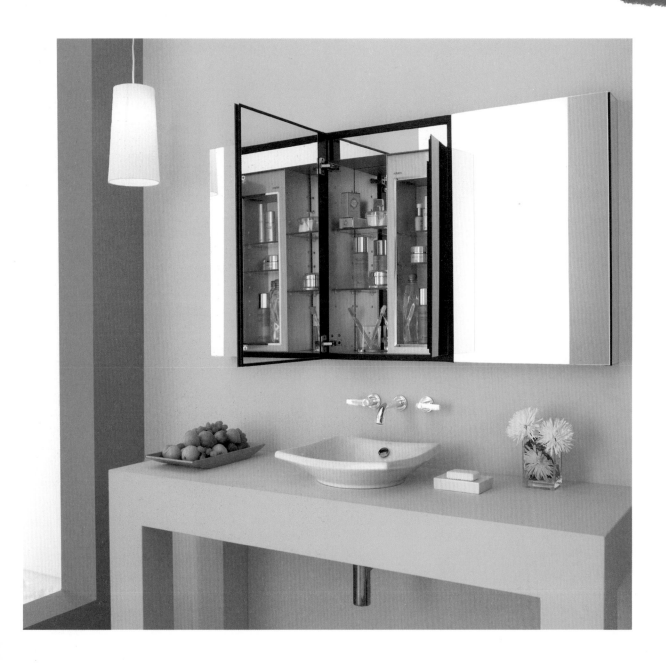

4	165
193	195

LEFT The rich terracotta of the walls create a cosy bathing environment. The crisp white of the basin and towel coupled with the steely blue opaque glass prevent the room becoming too dark and overpowering.

1	58
56	54

RIGHT Rich dark reds have a timeless quality, which when combined with strong browns of the wood and the cushions, and set off by the neutral sofa covering, produce an elegant contemporary living space.

3	141	2	91
137	143	93	56

BELOW By using many neutral colors this scheme conveys an immediate impression of calm. The accent colors are provided by the thriving plants which also add to the ambience.

RIGHT Strong pinks can be overpowering but when combined with other rich colors such as purple, create a feeling of opulence.

ultra violet 7

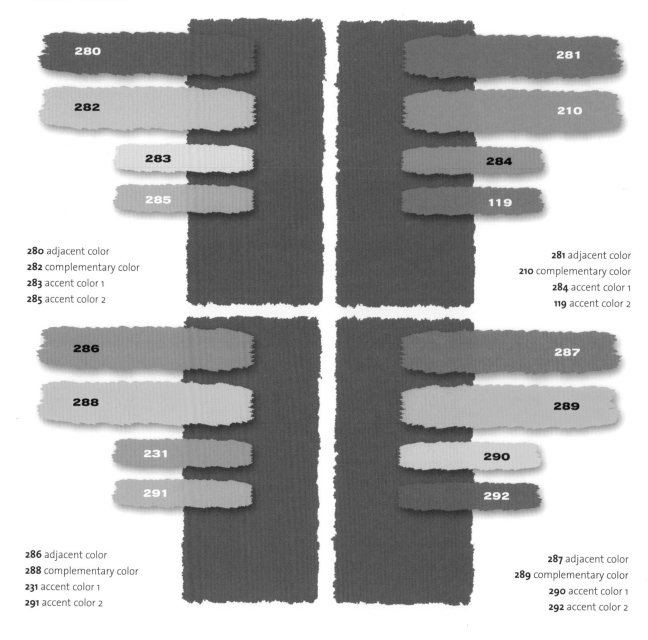

280 adjacent color
282 complementary color
283 accent color 1
285 accent color 2

281 adjacent color
210 complementary color
284 accent color 1
119 accent color 2

286 adjacent color
288 complementary color
231 accent color 1
291 accent color 2

287 adjacent color
289 complementary color
290 accent color 1
292 accent color 2

ultra violet 7

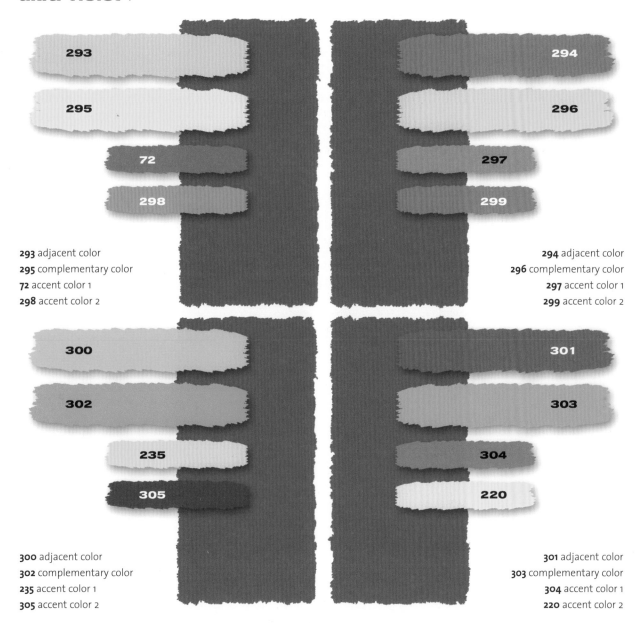

293 adjacent color
295 complementary color
72 accent color 1
298 accent color 2

294 adjacent color
296 complementary color
297 accent color 1
299 accent color 2

300 adjacent color
302 complementary color
235 accent color 1
305 accent color 2

301 adjacent color
303 complementary color
304 accent color 1
220 accent color 2

ultra violet 7

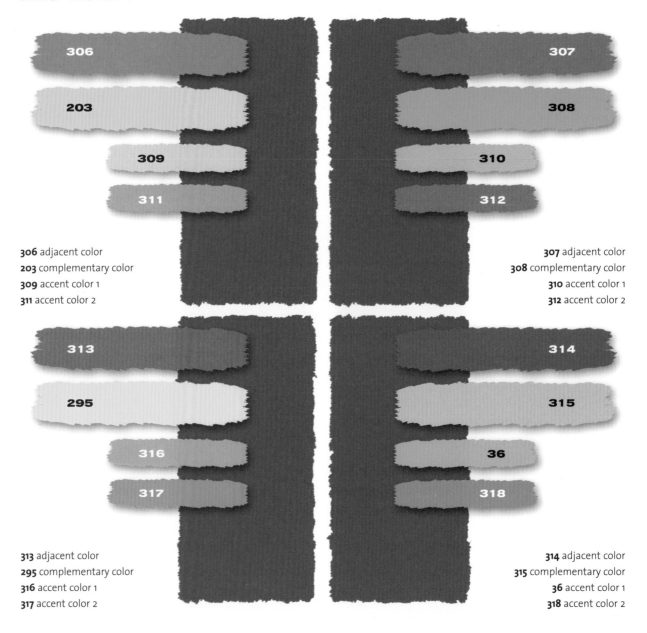

306 adjacent color
203 complementary color
309 accent color 1
311 accent color 2

307 adjacent color
308 complementary color
310 accent color 1
312 accent color 2

313 adjacent color
295 complementary color
316 accent color 1
317 accent color 2

314 adjacent color
315 complementary color
36 accent color 1
318 accent color 2

burnt sienna 8

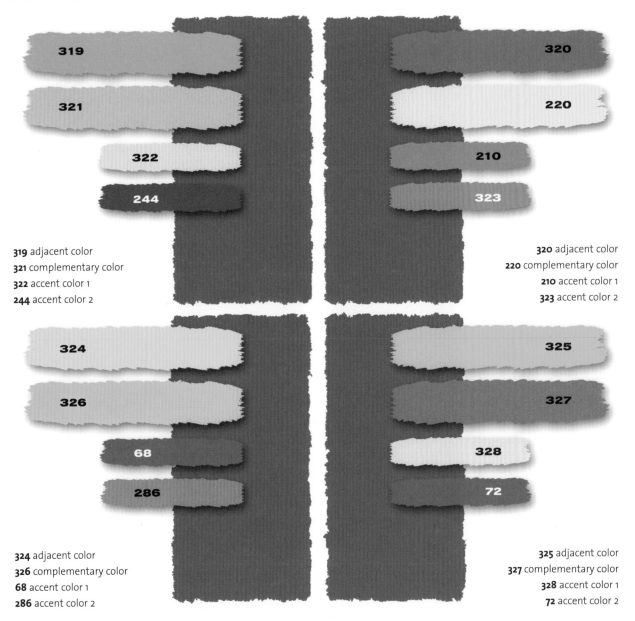

319 adjacent color
321 complementary color
322 accent color 1
244 accent color 2

320 adjacent color
220 complementary color
210 accent color 1
323 accent color 2

324 adjacent color
326 complementary color
68 accent color 1
286 accent color 2

325 adjacent color
327 complementary color
328 accent color 1
72 accent color 2

burnt sienna 8

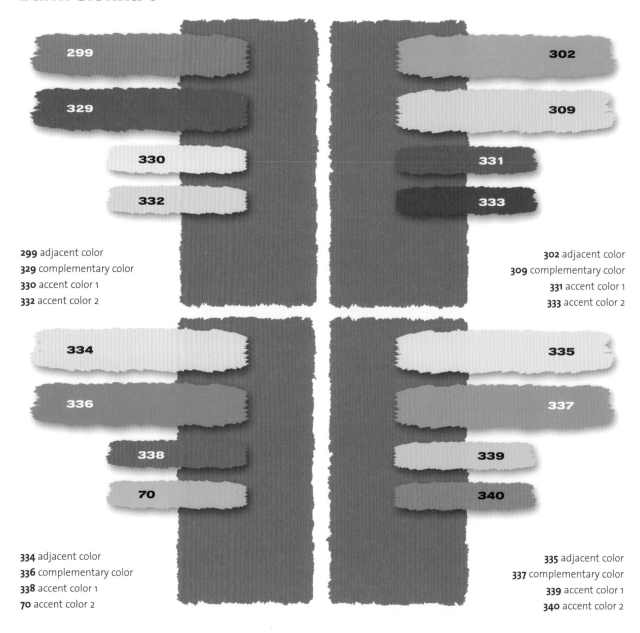

299 adjacent color
329 complementary color
330 accent color 1
332 accent color 2

302 adjacent color
309 complementary color
331 accent color 1
333 accent color 2

334 adjacent color
336 complementary color
338 accent color 1
70 accent color 2

335 adjacent color
337 complementary color
339 accent color 1
340 accent color 2

burnt sienna 8

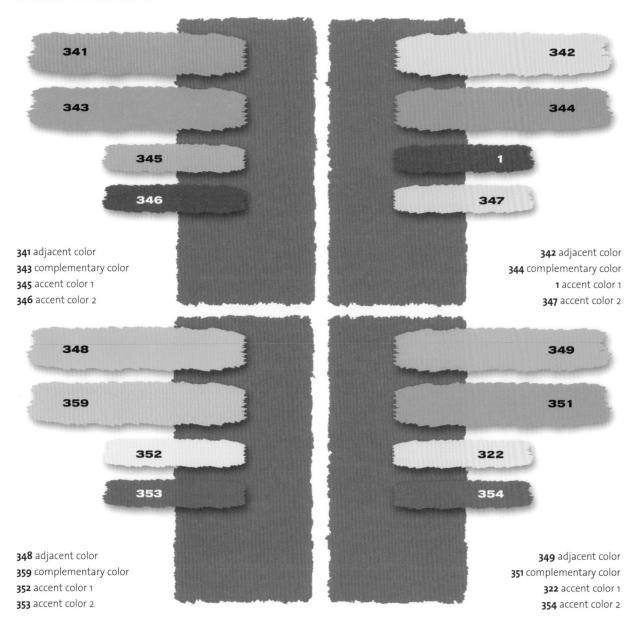

341 adjacent color
343 complementary color
345 accent color 1
346 accent color 2

342 adjacent color
344 complementary color
1 accent color 1
347 accent color 2

348 adjacent color
359 complementary color
352 accent color 1
353 accent color 2

349 adjacent color
351 complementary color
322 accent color 1
354 accent color 2

paris romance 9

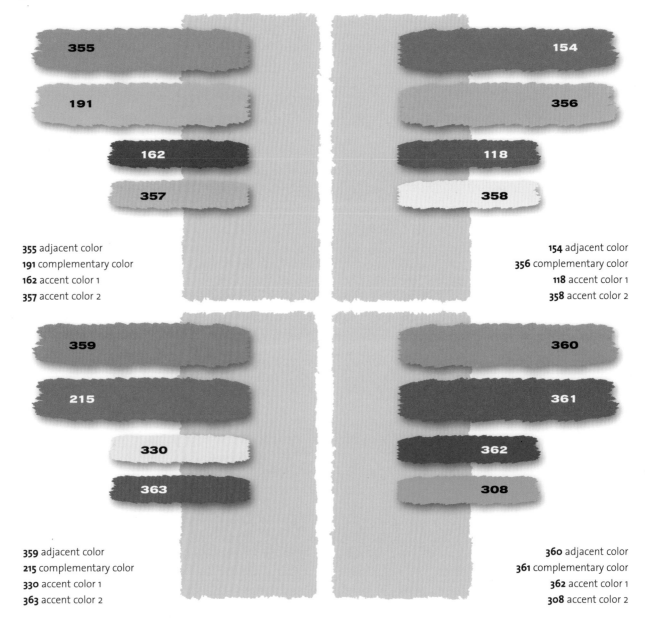

355 adjacent color
191 complementary color
162 accent color 1
357 accent color 2

154 adjacent color
356 complementary color
118 accent color 1
358 accent color 2

359 adjacent color
215 complementary color
330 accent color 1
363 accent color 2

360 adjacent color
361 complementary color
362 accent color 1
308 accent color 2

paris romance 9

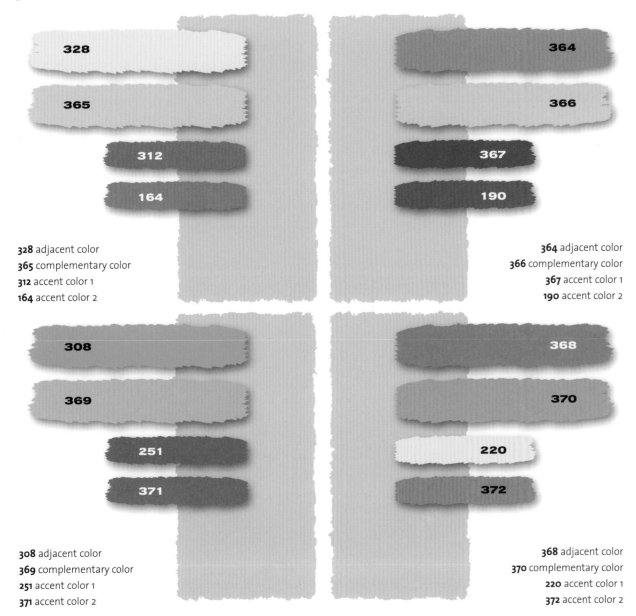

328 adjacent color
365 complementary color
312 accent color 1
164 accent color 2

364 adjacent color
366 complementary color
367 accent color 1
190 accent color 2

308 adjacent color
369 complementary color
251 accent color 1
371 accent color 2

368 adjacent color
370 complementary color
220 accent color 1
372 accent color 2

paris romance 9

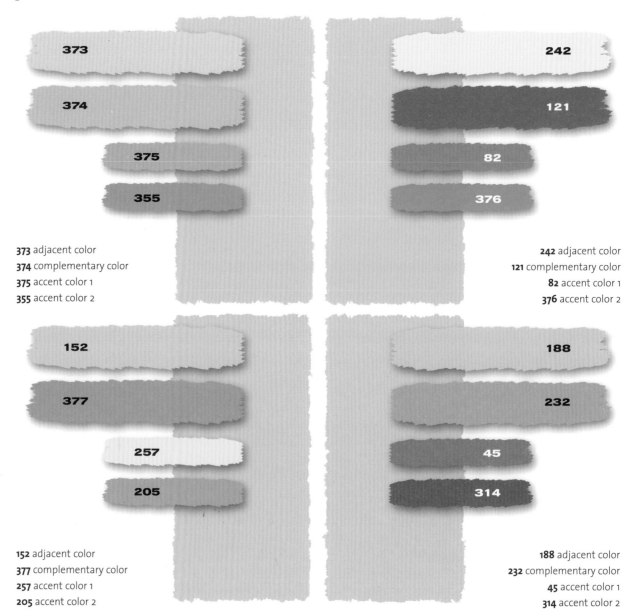

373
374
375
355

242
121
82
376

152
377
257
205

188
232
45
314

373 adjacent color
374 complementary color
375 accent color 1
355 accent color 2

242 adjacent color
121 complementary color
82 accent color 1
376 accent color 2

152 adjacent color
377 complementary color
257 accent color 1
205 accent color 2

188 adjacent color
232 complementary color
45 accent color 1
314 accent color 2

tucson tan 10

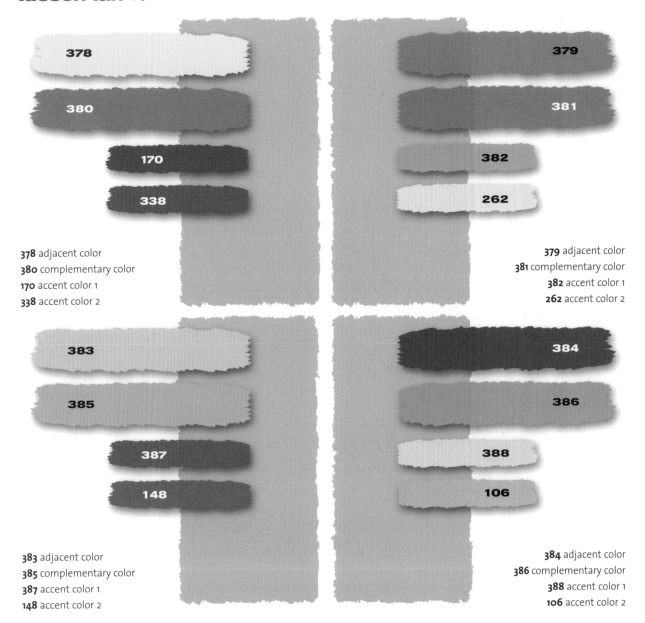

378 adjacent color
380 complementary color
170 accent color 1
338 accent color 2

379 adjacent color
381 complementary color
382 accent color 1
262 accent color 2

383 adjacent color
385 complementary color
387 accent color 1
148 accent color 2

384 adjacent color
386 complementary color
388 accent color 1
106 accent color 2

tucson tan 10

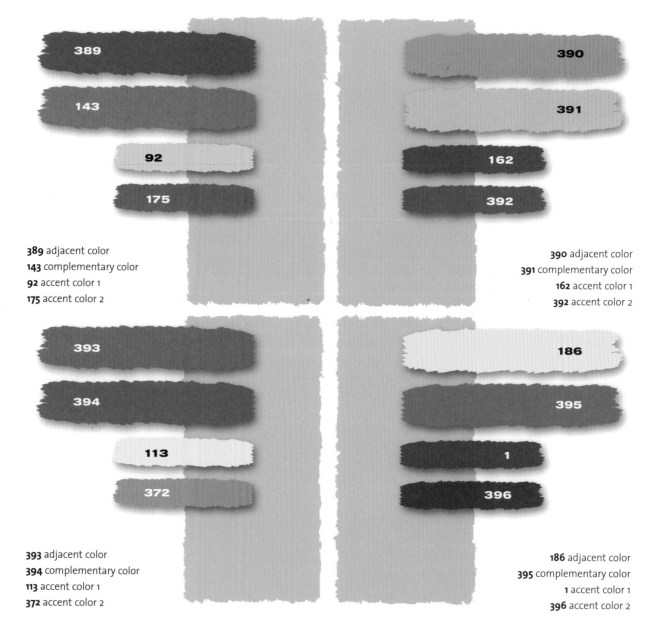

389 adjacent color
143 complementary color
92 accent color 1
175 accent color 2

390 adjacent color
391 complementary color
162 accent color 1
392 accent color 2

393 adjacent color
394 complementary color
113 accent color 1
372 accent color 2

186 adjacent color
395 complementary color
1 accent color 1
396 accent color 2

tucson tan 10

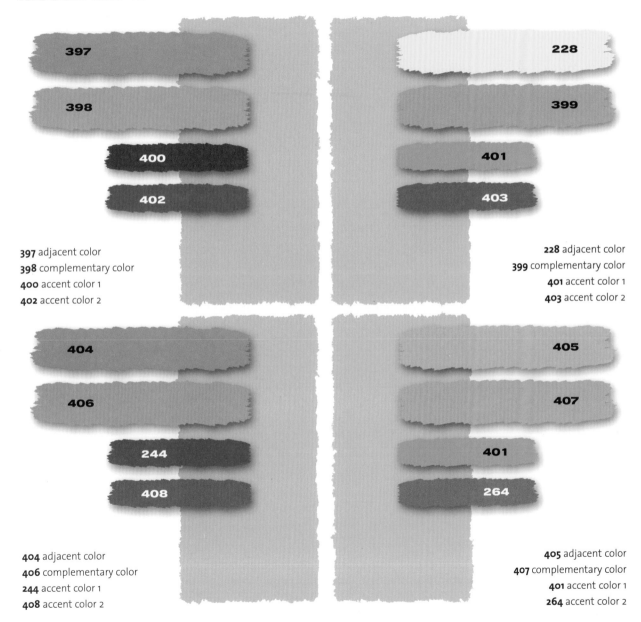

397 adjacent color
398 complementary color
400 accent color 1
402 accent color 2

228 adjacent color
399 complementary color
401 accent color 1
403 accent color 2

404 adjacent color
406 complementary color
244 accent color 1
408 accent color 2

405 adjacent color
407 complementary color
401 accent color 1
264 accent color 2

freesia 11

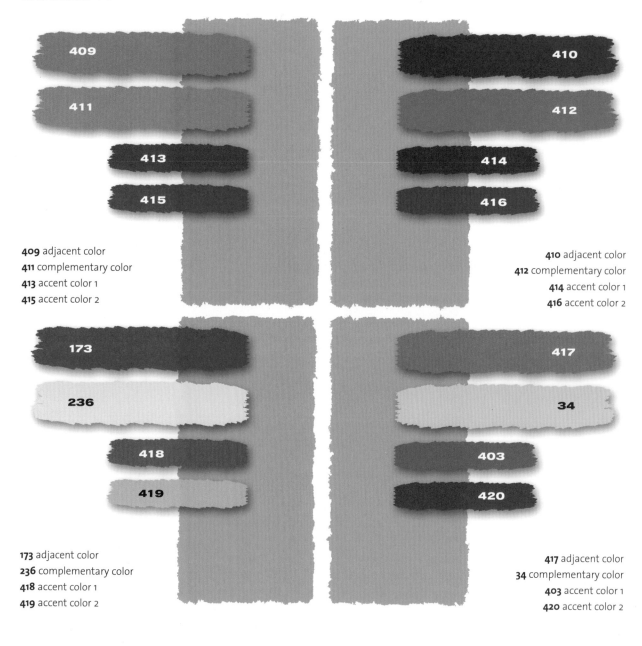

409 adjacent color
411 complementary color
413 accent color 1
415 accent color 2

410 adjacent color
412 complementary color
414 accent color 1
416 accent color 2

173 adjacent color
236 complementary color
418 accent color 1
419 accent color 2

417 adjacent color
34 complementary color
403 accent color 1
420 accent color 2

freesia 11

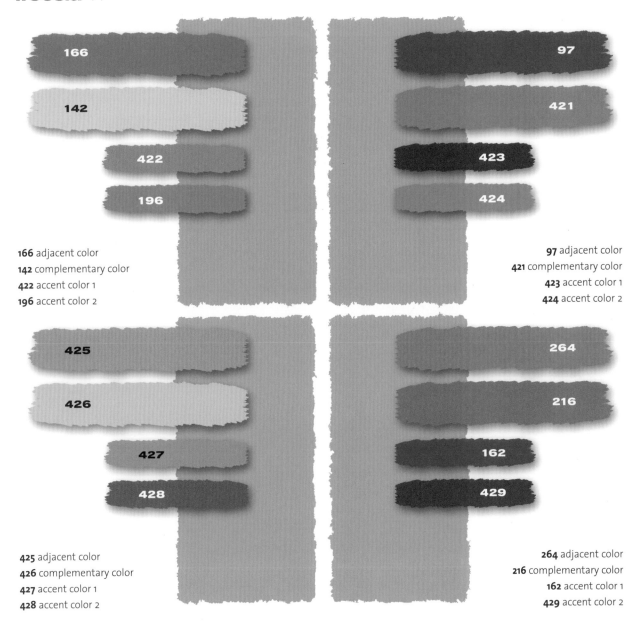

166 adjacent color
142 complementary color
422 accent color 1
196 accent color 2

97 adjacent color
421 complementary color
423 accent color 1
424 accent color 2

425 adjacent color
426 complementary color
427 accent color 1
428 accent color 2

264 adjacent color
216 complementary color
162 accent color 1
429 accent color 2

freesia 11

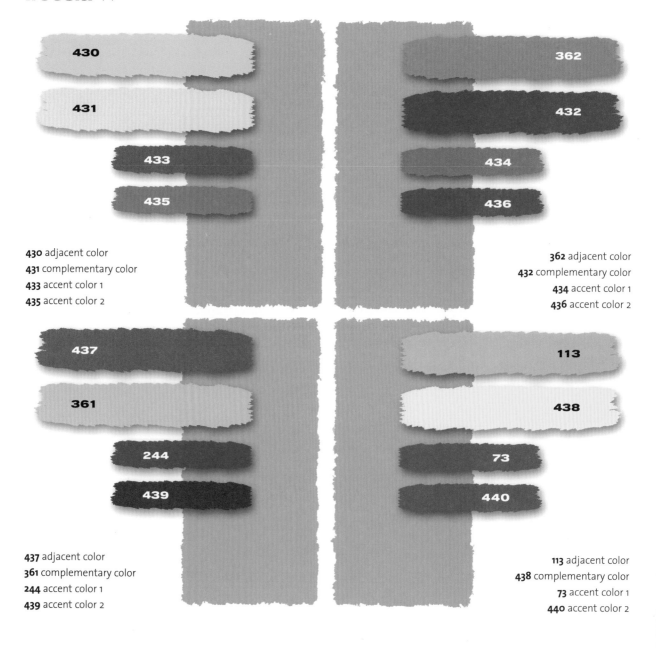

430 adjacent color
431 complementary color
433 accent color 1
435 accent color 2

362 adjacent color
432 complementary color
434 accent color 1
436 accent color 2

437 adjacent color
361 complementary color
244 accent color 1
439 accent color 2

113 adjacent color
438 complementary color
73 accent color 1
440 accent color 2

secret 12

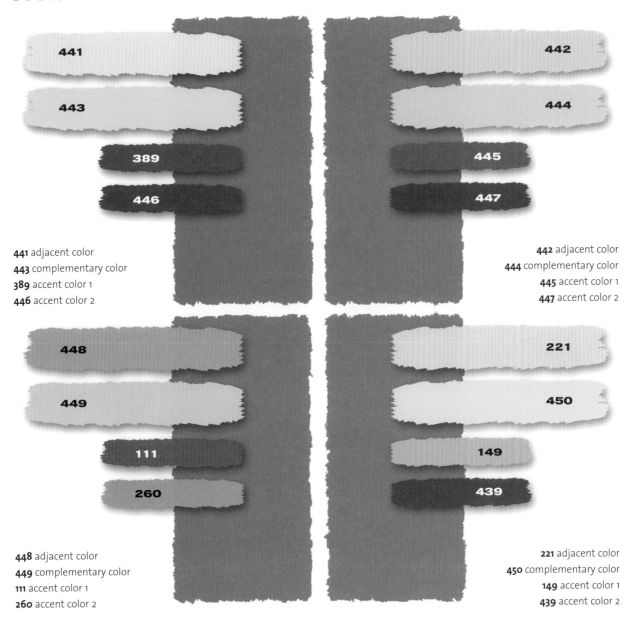

441
443
389
446

442
444
445
447

448
449
111
260

221
450
149
439

441 adjacent color
443 complementary color
389 accent color 1
446 accent color 2

442 adjacent color
444 complementary color
445 accent color 1
447 accent color 2

448 adjacent color
449 complementary color
111 accent color 1
260 accent color 2

221 adjacent color
450 complementary color
149 accent color 1
439 accent color 2

secret 12

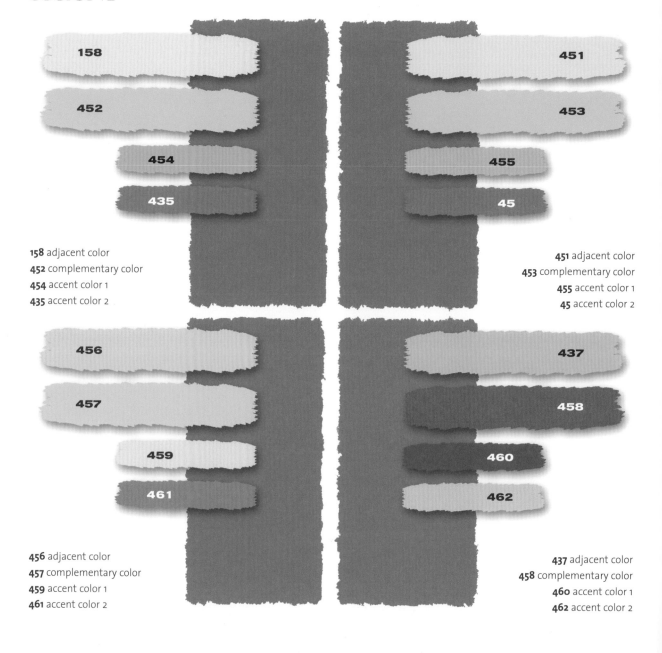

158 | 451

452 | 453

454 | 455

435 | 45

158 adjacent color
452 complementary color
454 accent color 1
435 accent color 2

451 adjacent color
453 complementary color
455 accent color 1
45 accent color 2

456 | 437

457 | 458

459 | 460

461 | 462

456 adjacent color
457 complementary color
459 accent color 1
461 accent color 2

437 adjacent color
458 complementary color
460 accent color 1
462 accent color 2

secret 12

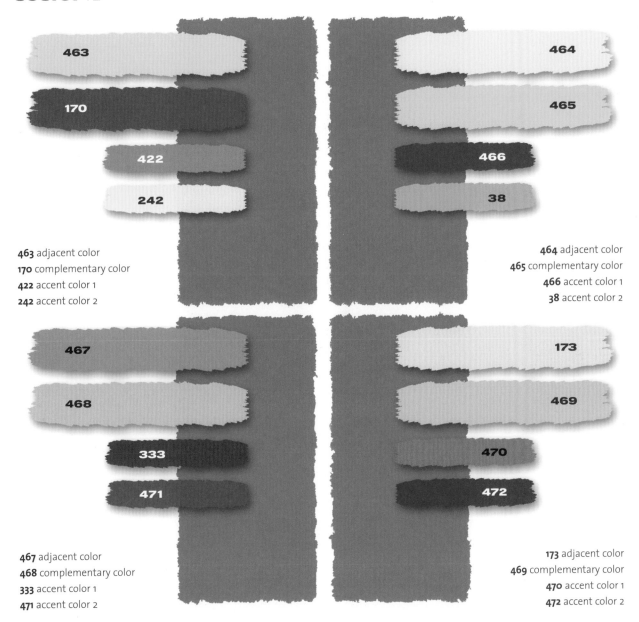

463 adjacent color
170 complementary color
422 accent color 1
242 accent color 2

464 adjacent color
465 complementary color
466 accent color 1
38 accent color 2

467 adjacent color
468 complementary color
333 accent color 1
471 accent color 2

173 adjacent color
469 complementary color
470 accent color 1
472 accent color 2

12	471
467	333

LEFT Gray is a much under-rated color. It has so many subtle variations of hue and tone that it can be used in any and every situation. Here the warm gray is the perfect backdrop for the strong color in the art and the soft furnishings.

7	302
300	235

RIGHT Strong saturated colors, such as purple and orange, used in contrast, create a space that is physically sensual and welcoming, and in addition stimulates mental activity.

215	385
468	871

12	221
439	450

ABOVE The clean lines and simple design of the bedside table and light sit in harmony with the neutral color scheme, providing a contemporary and sensual environment that will not dominate the room.

RIGHT The cool neutrals of the smooth walls and the reflections created in the polished floor help to create a beautiful contrast with the coarse textured deep indigo material covering the bench, and the rich green raw silk drapes, that makes for a totally relaxing experience.

9	359	10	387
215	330	148	383

BELOW With its use of granite, stainless steel and glass, set against the warm neutral color scheme, this kitchen provides the setting for a very sensual cooking and eating experience.

RIGHT The sombre tones of the sofa, cushions and floor covering are brought to life by the contrast with the rich salmon pink walls, giving this room its welcoming appeal.

splendor 13

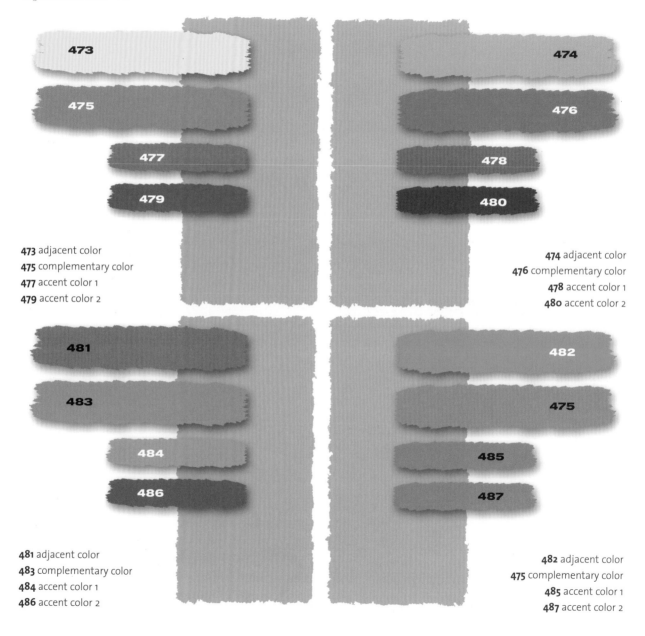

473 adjacent color
475 complementary color
477 accent color 1
479 accent color 2

474 adjacent color
476 complementary color
478 accent color 1
480 accent color 2

481 adjacent color
483 complementary color
484 accent color 1
486 accent color 2

482 adjacent color
475 complementary color
485 accent color 1
487 accent color 2

savannah clay 14

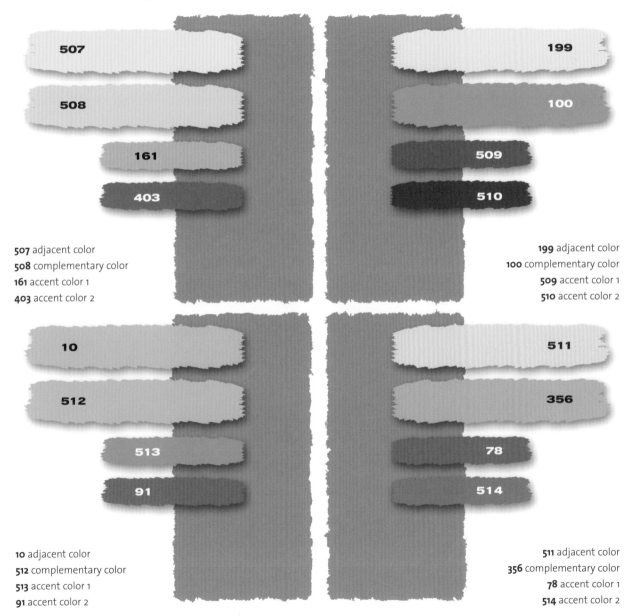

507 adjacent color
508 complementary color
161 accent color 1
403 accent color 2

199 adjacent color
100 complementary color
509 accent color 1
510 accent color 2

10 adjacent color
512 complementary color
513 accent color 1
91 accent color 2

511 adjacent color
356 complementary color
78 accent color 1
514 accent color 2

savannah clay 14

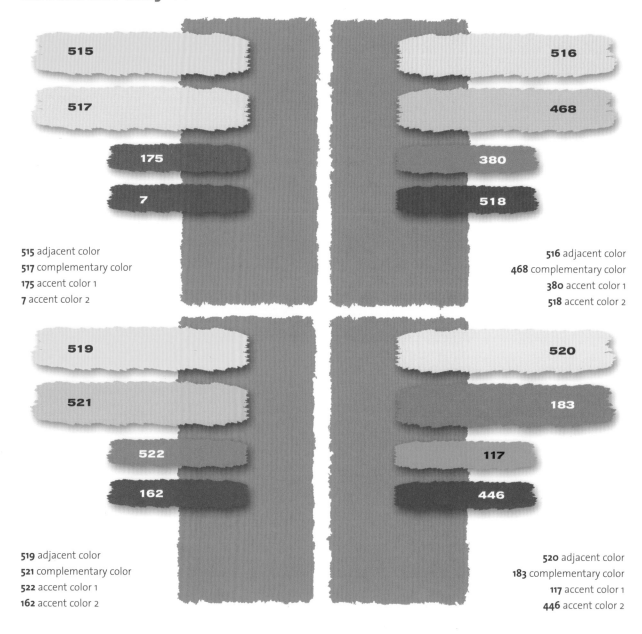

515
516
517
468
175
380
7
518

515 adjacent color
517 complementary color
175 accent color 1
7 accent color 2

516 adjacent color
468 complementary color
380 accent color 1
518 accent color 2

519
520
521
183
522
117
162
446

519 adjacent color
521 complementary color
522 accent color 1
162 accent color 2

520 adjacent color
183 complementary color
117 accent color 1
446 accent color 2

savannah clay 14

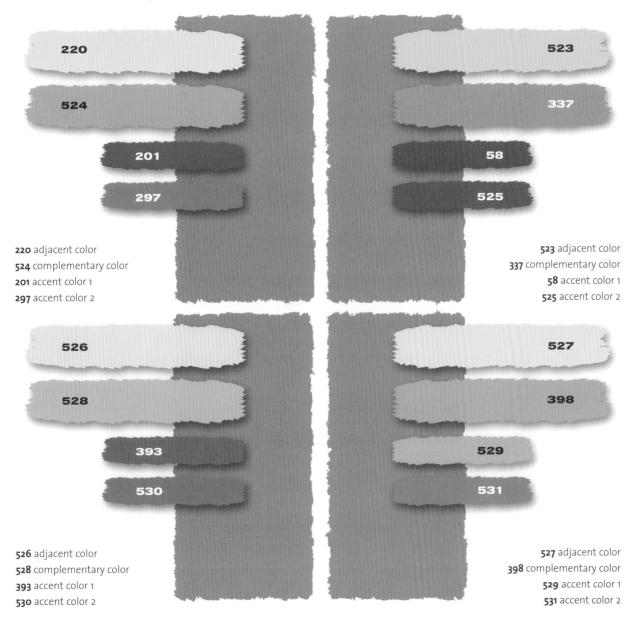

220 adjacent color
524 complementary color
201 accent color 1
297 accent color 2

523 adjacent color
337 complementary color
58 accent color 1
525 accent color 2

526 adjacent color
528 complementary color
393 accent color 1
530 accent color 2

527 adjacent color
398 complementary color
529 accent color 1
531 accent color 2

meadow pink 15

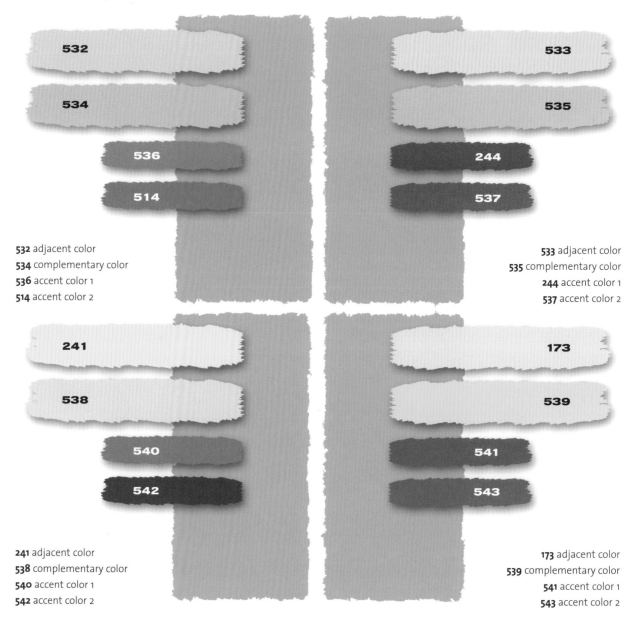

532

534

536

514

533

535

244

537

532 adjacent color
534 complementary color
536 accent color 1
514 accent color 2

533 adjacent color
535 complementary color
244 accent color 1
537 accent color 2

241

538

540

542

173

539

541

543

241 adjacent color
538 complementary color
540 accent color 1
542 accent color 2

173 adjacent color
539 complementary color
541 accent color 1
543 accent color 2

meadow pink 15

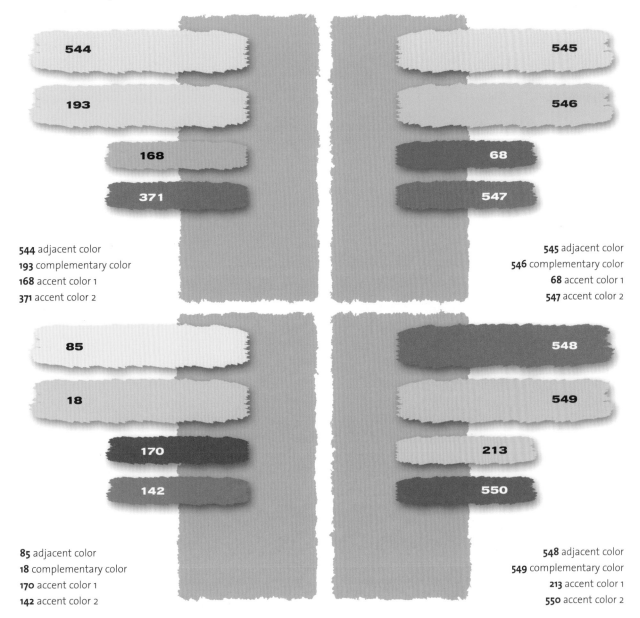

544 adjacent color
193 complementary color
168 accent color 1
371 accent color 2

545 adjacent color
546 complementary color
68 accent color 1
547 accent color 2

85 adjacent color
18 complementary color
170 accent color 1
142 accent color 2

548 adjacent color
549 complementary color
213 accent color 1
550 accent color 2

meadow pink 15

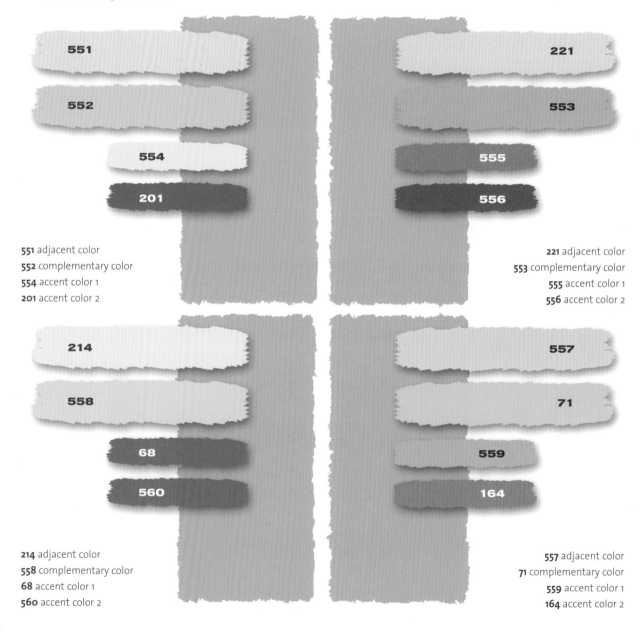

551 adjacent color
552 complementary color
554 accent color 1
201 accent color 2

221 adjacent color
553 complementary color
555 accent color 1
556 accent color 2

214 adjacent color
558 complementary color
68 accent color 1
560 accent color 2

557 adjacent color
71 complementary color
559 accent color 1
164 accent color 2

north cascades 16

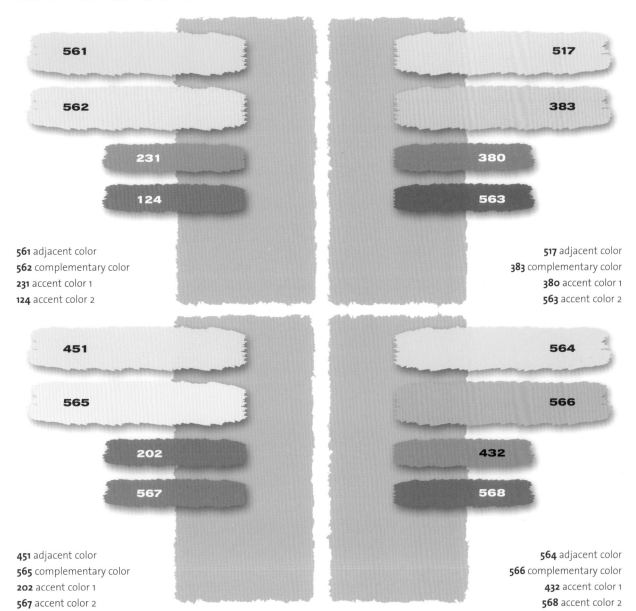

561 adjacent color
562 complementary color
231 accent color 1
124 accent color 2

517 adjacent color
383 complementary color
380 accent color 1
563 accent color 2

451 adjacent color
565 complementary color
202 accent color 1
567 accent color 2

564 adjacent color
566 complementary color
432 accent color 1
568 accent color 2

north cascades 16

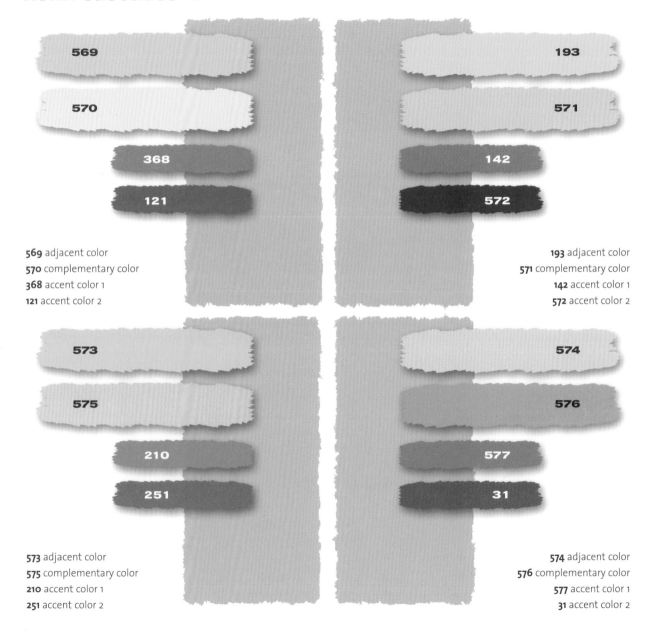

569

570

368

121

193

571

142

572

573

575

210

251

574

576

577

31

569 adjacent color
570 complementary color
368 accent color 1
121 accent color 2

193 adjacent color
571 complementary color
142 accent color 1
572 accent color 2

573 adjacent color
575 complementary color
210 accent color 1
251 accent color 2

574 adjacent color
576 complementary color
577 accent color 1
31 accent color 2

north cascades 16

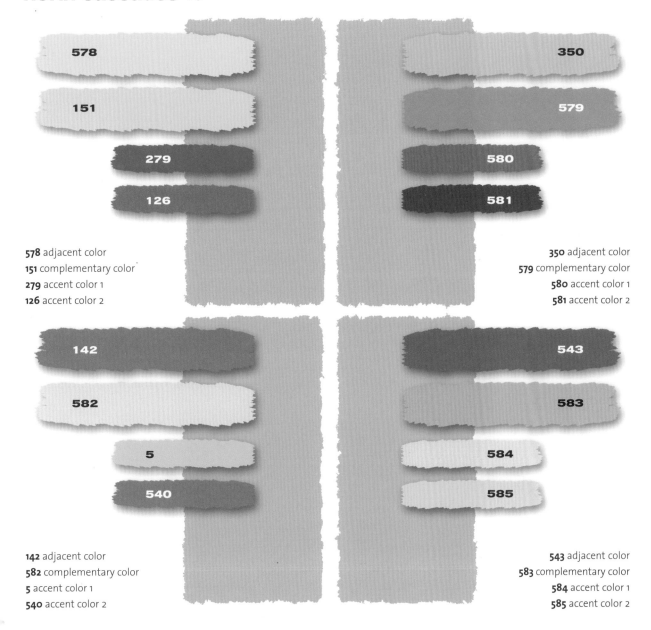

578 adjacent color
151 complementary color
279 accent color 1
126 accent color 2

350 adjacent color
579 complementary color
580 accent color 1
581 accent color 2

142 adjacent color
582 complementary color
5 accent color 1
540 accent color 2

543 adjacent color
583 complementary color
584 accent color 1
585 accent color 2

wispy green 17

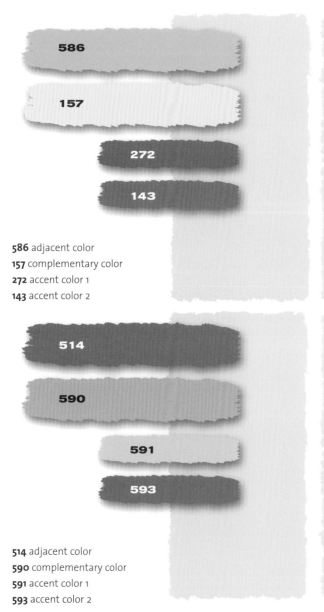

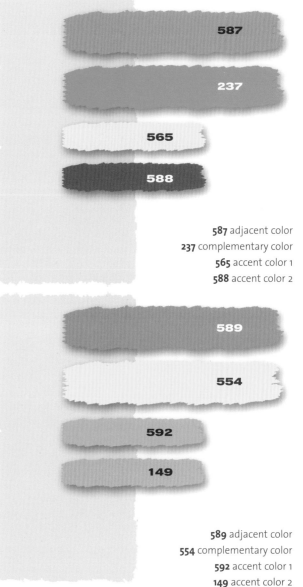

586 adjacent color
157 complementary color
272 accent color 1
143 accent color 2

587 adjacent color
237 complementary color
565 accent color 1
588 accent color 2

514 adjacent color
590 complementary color
591 accent color 1
593 accent color 2

589 adjacent color
554 complementary color
592 accent color 1
149 accent color 2

wispy green 17

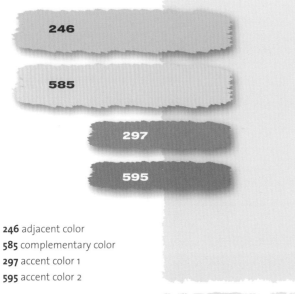

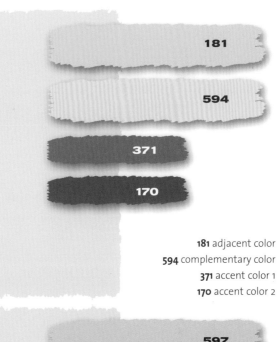

246 adjacent color
585 complementary color
297 accent color 1
595 accent color 2

181 adjacent color
594 complementary color
371 accent color 1
170 accent color 2

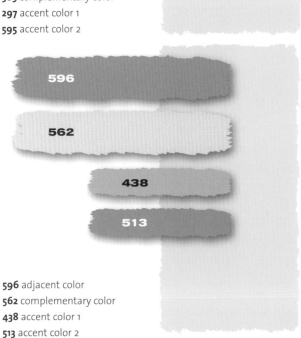

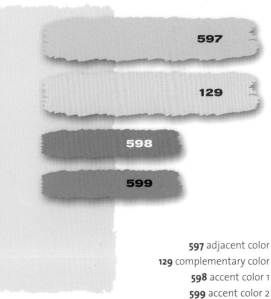

596 adjacent color
562 complementary color
438 accent color 1
513 accent color 2

597 adjacent color
129 complementary color
598 accent color 1
599 accent color 2

wispy green 17

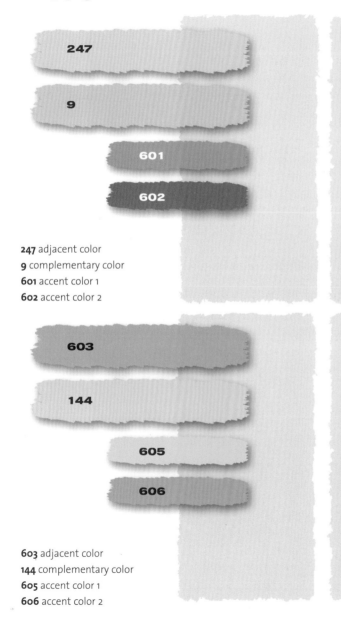

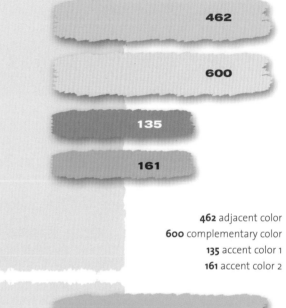

247
9
601
602

462
600
135
161

247 adjacent color
9 complementary color
601 accent color 1
602 accent color 2

462 adjacent color
600 complementary color
135 accent color 1
161 accent color 2

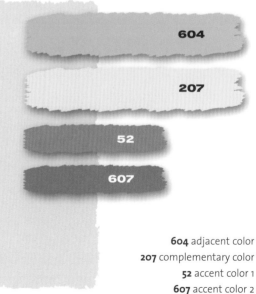

603
144
605
606

604
207
52
607

603 adjacent color
144 complementary color
605 accent color 1
606 accent color 2

604 adjacent color
207 complementary color
52 accent color 1
607 accent color 2

violet mist 18

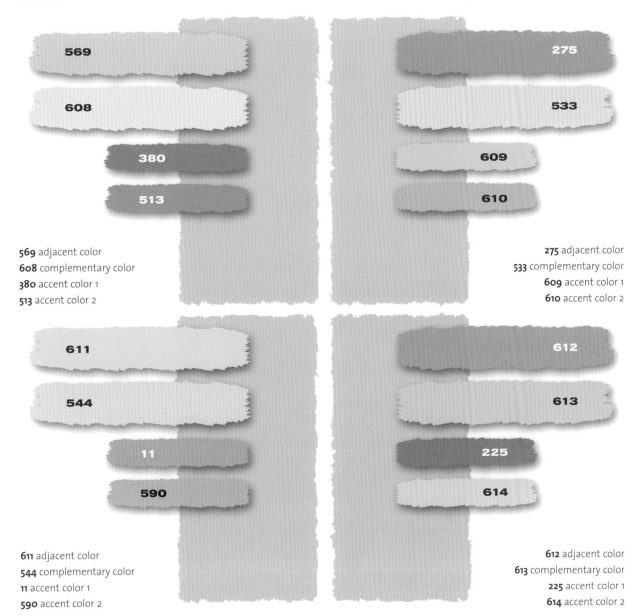

569 adjacent color
608 complementary color
380 accent color 1
513 accent color 2

275 adjacent color
533 complementary color
609 accent color 1
610 accent color 2

611 adjacent color
544 complementary color
11 accent color 1
590 accent color 2

612 adjacent color
613 complementary color
225 accent color 1
614 accent color 2

violet mist 18

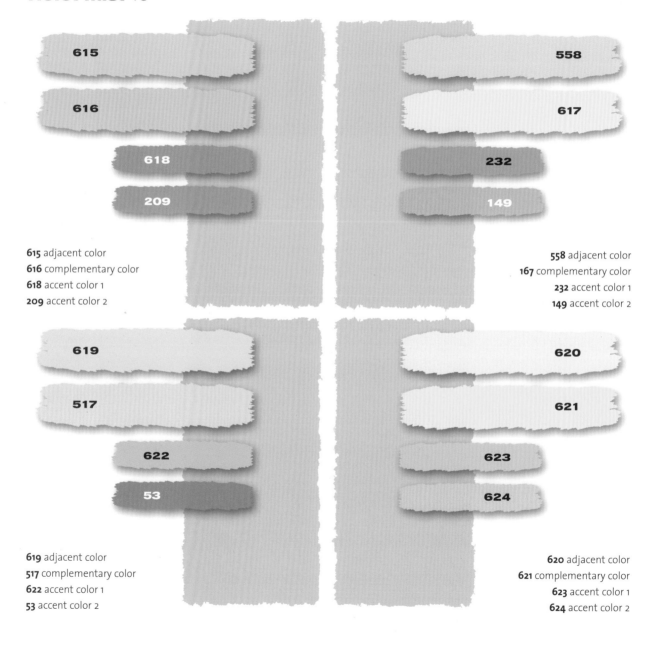

615

616

618

209

558

617

232

149

615 adjacent color
616 complementary color
618 accent color 1
209 accent color 2

558 adjacent color
167 complementary color
232 accent color 1
149 accent color 2

619

517

622

53

620

621

623

624

619 adjacent color
517 complementary color
622 accent color 1
53 accent color 2

620 adjacent color
621 complementary color
623 accent color 1
624 accent color 2

violet mist 18

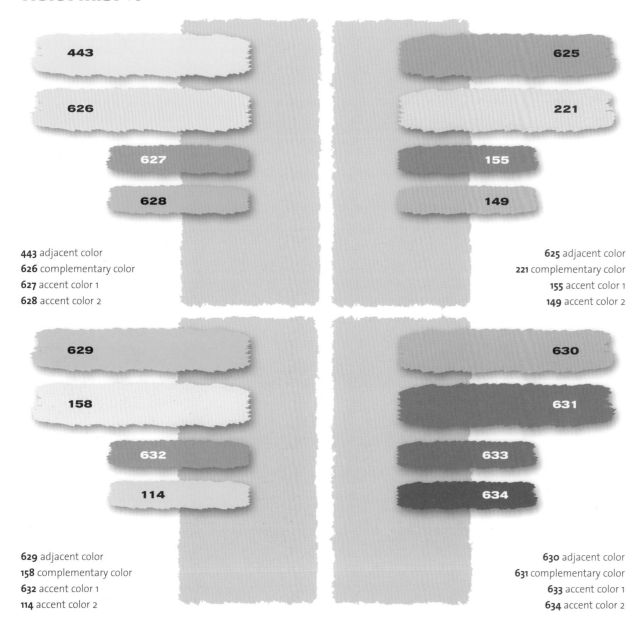

443 adjacent color
626 complementary color
627 accent color 1
628 accent color 2

625 adjacent color
221 complementary color
155 accent color 1
149 accent color 2

629 adjacent color
158 complementary color
632 accent color 1
114 accent color 2

630 adjacent color
631 complementary color
633 accent color 1
634 accent color 2

16	121	414	554
569	570	149	592

BELOW Using a cool neutral color in this kitchen, helps to bring out the natural richness of the wooden cabinets and the stone worktops.

RIGHT A bright fresh bedroom using a cool green contrasted with the rich golden glow of the cushions preventing it from appearing too cold.

414	871
592	569

RIGHT Keeping the color scheme clean and simple makes for a space that is calm and peaceful, and that will benefit from small touches of accent color. Here the flowing lines of the vases soften the strong angular shapes of the television and shelving units.

18	149
121	570

LEFT Even small touches of accent color, such as these bright red, orange, and yellow lamp shades, have a dramatic effect on a room, here setting off the neutral walls and dark worktops.

15	16

RIGHT A color scheme which uses tones of the same hue is the ultimate in conveying tranquilty, everything works together to create a space that is gentle to the eye.

| 14 | 515 |
| 175 | 570 |

LEFT Using a variety of shades of adjacent colors this scheme conveys a sense of warmth, naturally drawing the eye to the contrasting shower, emphasized by daylight flooding in through a glass wall.

| 16 | 570 |
| 175 | 2 |

RIGHT A rich purple can be softened by using broken paint effects and paler tones. Combine this with dark woods and touches of white to create a hint of the exotic.

moroccan spice 19

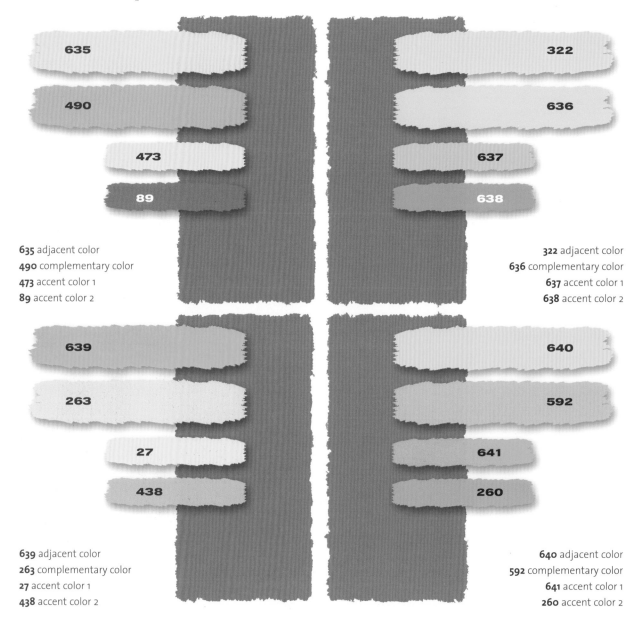

635 adjacent color
490 complementary color
473 accent color 1
89 accent color 2

322 adjacent color
636 complementary color
637 accent color 1
638 accent color 2

639 adjacent color
263 complementary color
27 accent color 1
438 accent color 2

640 adjacent color
592 complementary color
641 accent color 1
260 accent color 2

moroccan spice 19

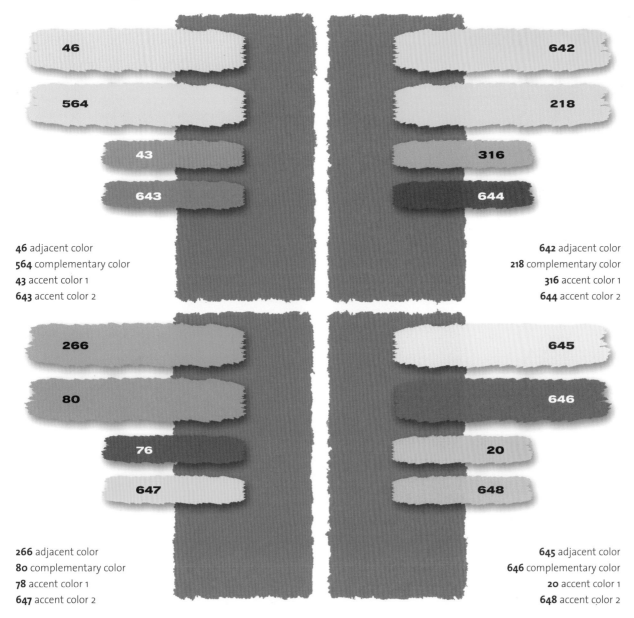

46 adjacent color
564 complementary color
43 accent color 1
643 accent color 2

642 adjacent color
218 complementary color
316 accent color 1
644 accent color 2

266 adjacent color
80 complementary color
78 accent color 1
647 accent color 2

645 adjacent color
646 complementary color
20 accent color 1
648 accent color 2

moroccan spice 19

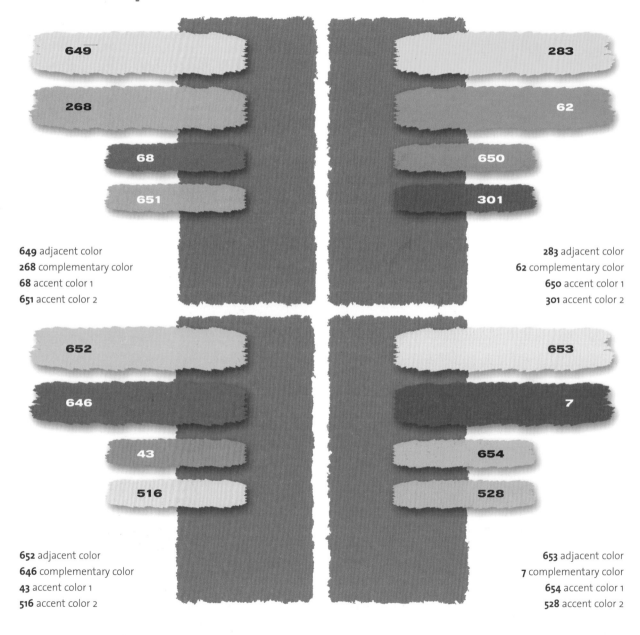

649 adjacent color
268 complementary color
68 accent color 1
651 accent color 2

283 adjacent color
62 complementary color
650 accent color 1
301 accent color 2

652 adjacent color
646 complementary color
43 accent color 1
516 accent color 2

653 adjacent color
7 complementary color
654 accent color 1
528 accent color 2

sunrays 20

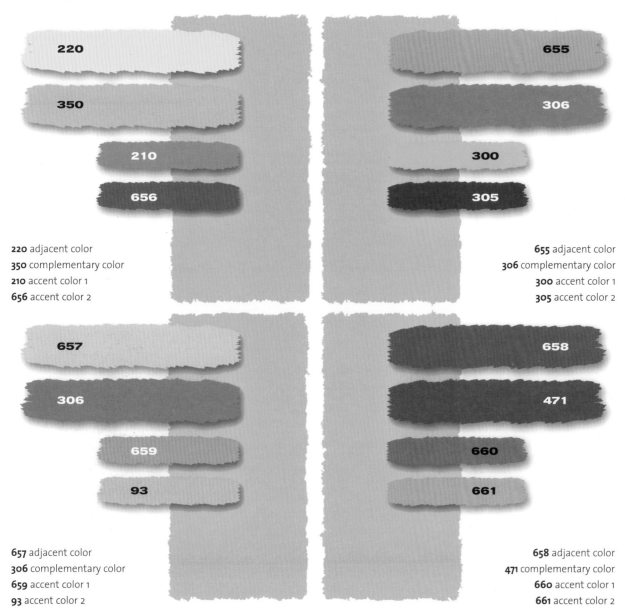

220 adjacent color
350 complementary color
210 accent color 1
656 accent color 2

655 adjacent color
306 complementary color
300 accent color 1
305 accent color 2

657 adjacent color
306 complementary color
659 accent color 1
93 accent color 2

658 adjacent color
471 complementary color
660 accent color 1
661 accent color 2

sunrays 20

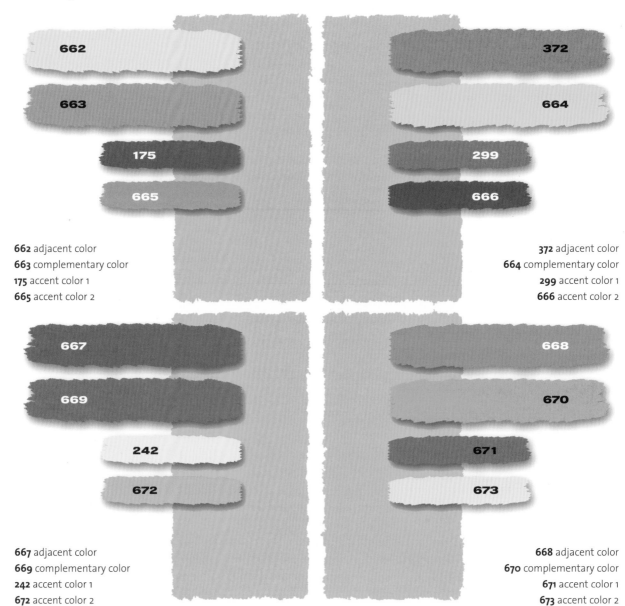

662 adjacent color
663 complementary color
175 accent color 1
665 accent color 2

372 adjacent color
664 complementary color
299 accent color 1
666 accent color 2

667 adjacent color
669 complementary color
242 accent color 1
672 accent color 2

668 adjacent color
670 complementary color
671 accent color 1
673 accent color 2

sunrays 20

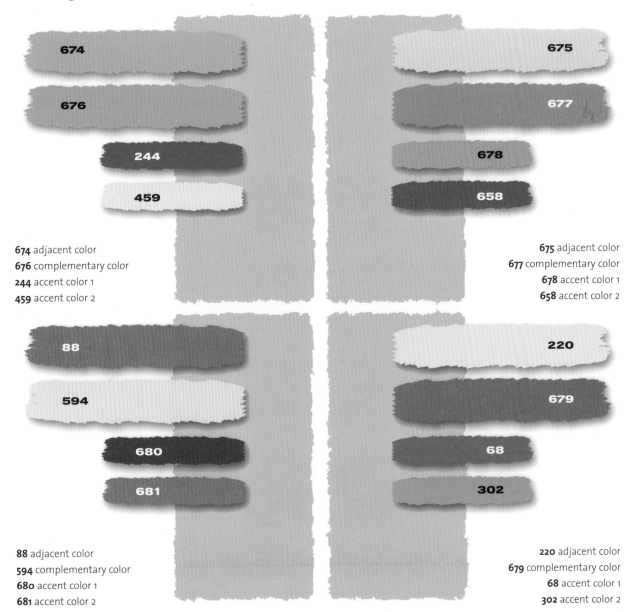

674
676
244
459

675
677
678
658

674 adjacent color
676 complementary color
244 accent color 1
459 accent color 2

675 adjacent color
677 complementary color
678 accent color 1
658 accent color 2

88
594
680
681

220
679
68
302

88 adjacent color
594 complementary color
680 accent color 1
681 accent color 2

220 adjacent color
679 complementary color
68 accent color 1
302 accent color 2

nova scotia blue 21

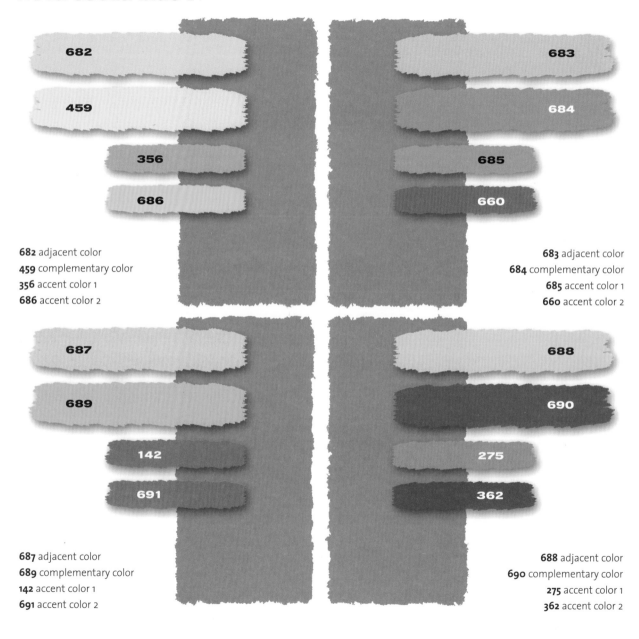

682 adjacent color
459 complementary color
356 accent color 1
686 accent color 2

683 adjacent color
684 complementary color
685 accent color 1
660 accent color 2

687 adjacent color
689 complementary color
142 accent color 1
691 accent color 2

688 adjacent color
690 complementary color
275 accent color 1
362 accent color 2

nova scotia blue 21

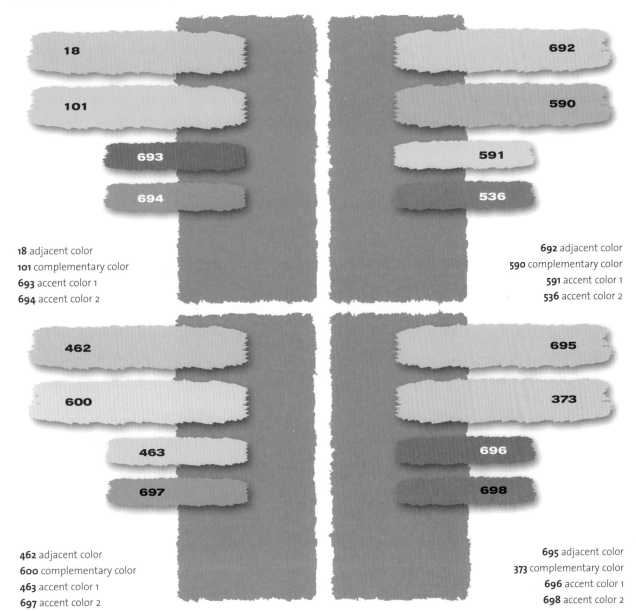

18 adjacent color
101 complementary color
693 accent color 1
694 accent color 2

692 adjacent color
590 complementary color
591 accent color 1
536 accent color 2

462 adjacent color
600 complementary color
463 accent color 1
697 accent color 2

695 adjacent color
373 complementary color
696 accent color 1
698 accent color 2

nova scotia blue 21

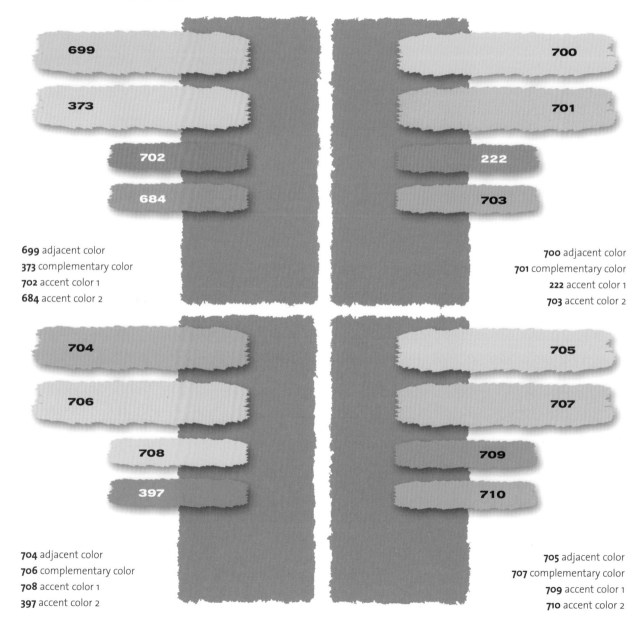

699 adjacent color
373 complementary color
702 accent color 1
684 accent color 2

700 adjacent color
701 complementary color
222 accent color 1
703 accent color 2

704 adjacent color
706 complementary color
708 accent color 1
397 accent color 2

705 adjacent color
707 complementary color
709 accent color 1
710 accent color 2

warm apple crisp 22

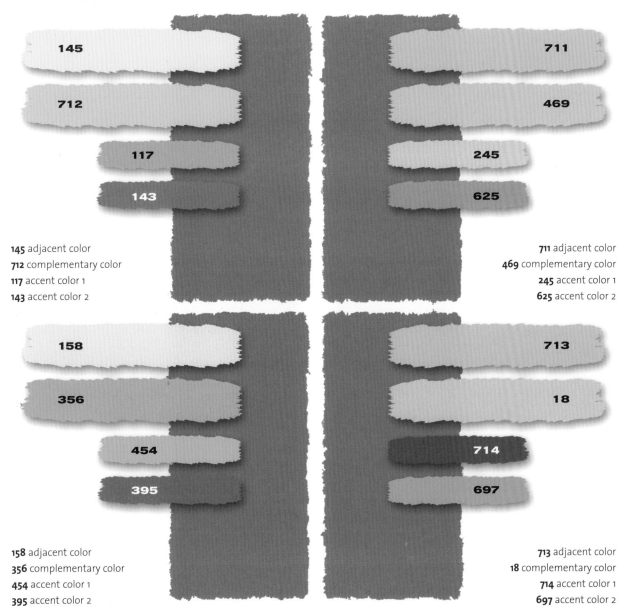

145 adjacent color
712 complementary color
117 accent color 1
143 accent color 2

711 adjacent color
469 complementary color
245 accent color 1
625 accent color 2

158 adjacent color
356 complementary color
454 accent color 1
395 accent color 2

713 adjacent color
18 complementary color
714 accent color 1
697 accent color 2

warm apple crisp 22

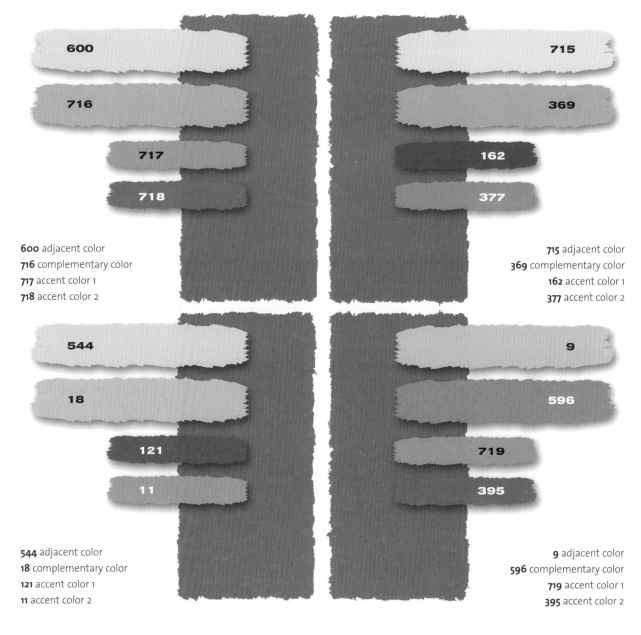

600
716
717
718

715
369
162
377

544
18
121
11

9
596
719
395

600 adjacent color
716 complementary color
717 accent color 1
718 accent color 2

715 adjacent color
369 complementary color
162 accent color 1
377 accent color 2

544 adjacent color
18 complementary color
121 accent color 1
11 accent color 2

9 adjacent color
596 complementary color
719 accent color 1
395 accent color 2

warm apple crisp 22

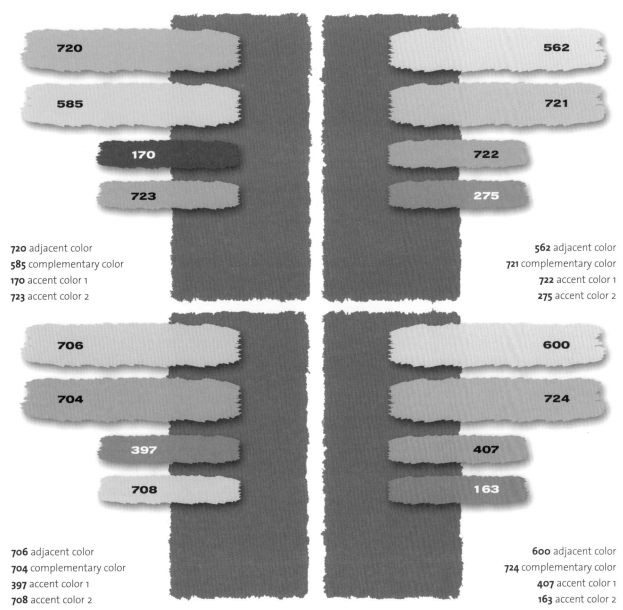

720 adjacent color
585 complementary color
170 accent color 1
723 accent color 2

562 adjacent color
721 complementary color
722 accent color 1
275 accent color 2

706 adjacent color
704 complementary color
397 accent color 1
708 accent color 2

600 adjacent color
724 complementary color
407 accent color 1
163 accent color 2

lemon grass 23

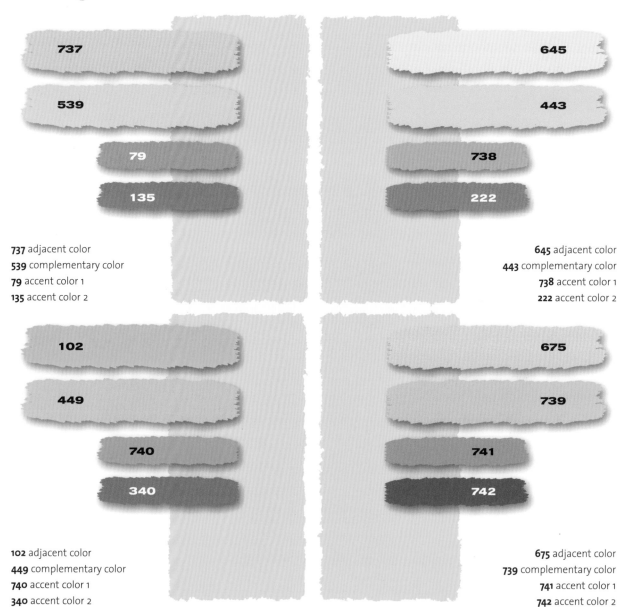

737 adjacent color
539 complementary color
79 accent color 1
135 accent color 2

645 adjacent color
443 complementary color
738 accent color 1
222 accent color 2

102 adjacent color
449 complementary color
740 accent color 1
340 accent color 2

675 adjacent color
739 complementary color
741 accent color 1
742 accent color 2

lemon grass 23

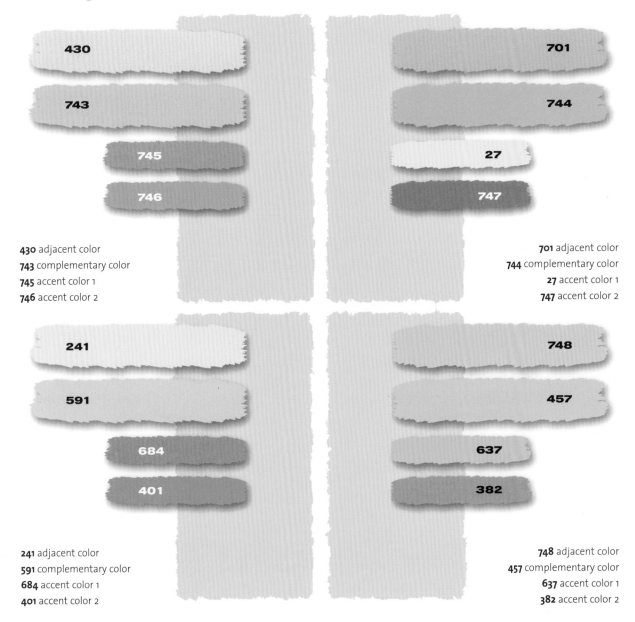

430 adjacent color
743 complementary color
745 accent color 1
746 accent color 2

701 adjacent color
744 complementary color
27 accent color 1
747 accent color 2

241 adjacent color
591 complementary color
684 accent color 1
401 accent color 2

748 adjacent color
457 complementary color
637 accent color 1
382 accent color 2

lemon grass 23

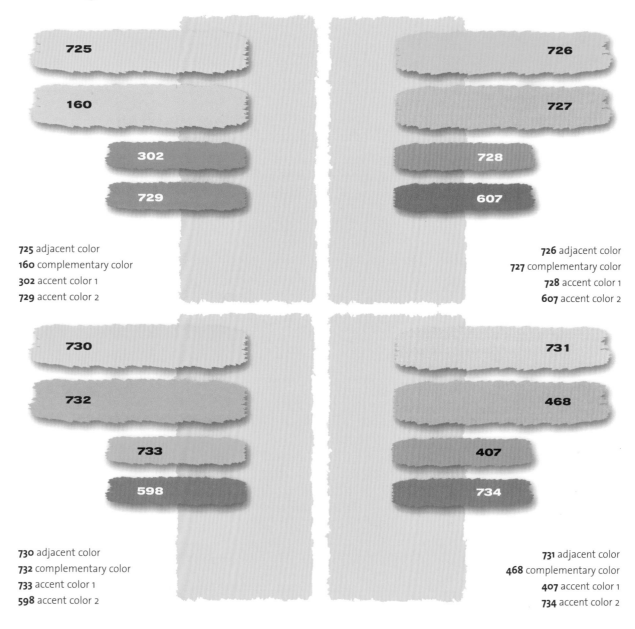

725 adjacent color
160 complementary color
302 accent color 1
729 accent color 2

726 adjacent color
727 complementary color
728 accent color 1
607 accent color 2

730 adjacent color
732 complementary color
733 accent color 1
598 accent color 2

731 adjacent color
468 complementary color
407 accent color 1
734 accent color 2

chic lime 24

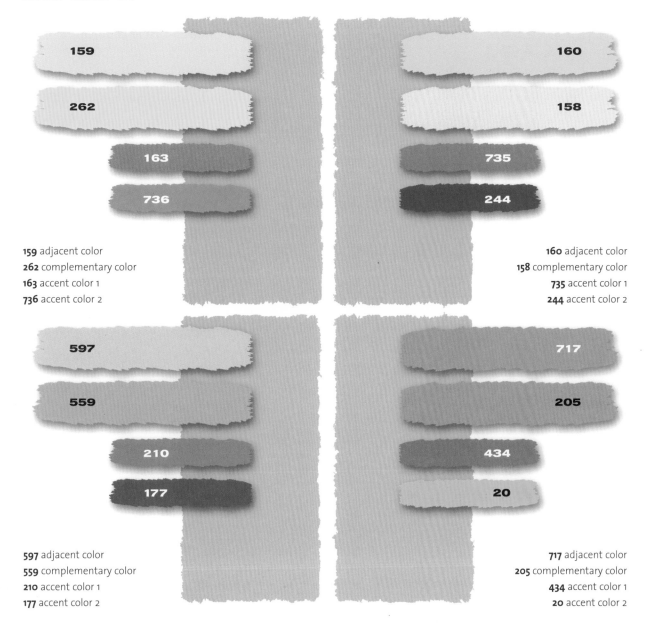

159	**160**
262	**158**
163	**735**
736	**244**

159 adjacent color
262 complementary color
163 accent color 1
736 accent color 2

160 adjacent color
158 complementary color
735 accent color 1
244 accent color 2

597	**717**
559	**205**
210	**434**
177	**20**

597 adjacent color
559 complementary color
210 accent color 1
177 accent color 2

717 adjacent color
205 complementary color
434 accent color 1
20 accent color 2

chic lime 24

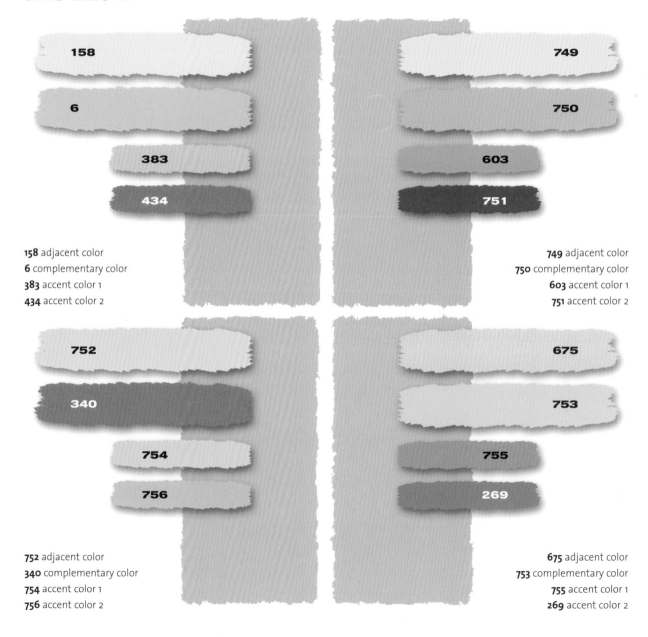

158 adjacent color
6 complementary color
383 accent color 1
434 accent color 2

749 adjacent color
750 complementary color
603 accent color 1
751 accent color 2

752 adjacent color
340 complementary color
754 accent color 1
756 accent color 2

675 adjacent color
753 complementary color
755 accent color 1
269 accent color 2

chic lime 24

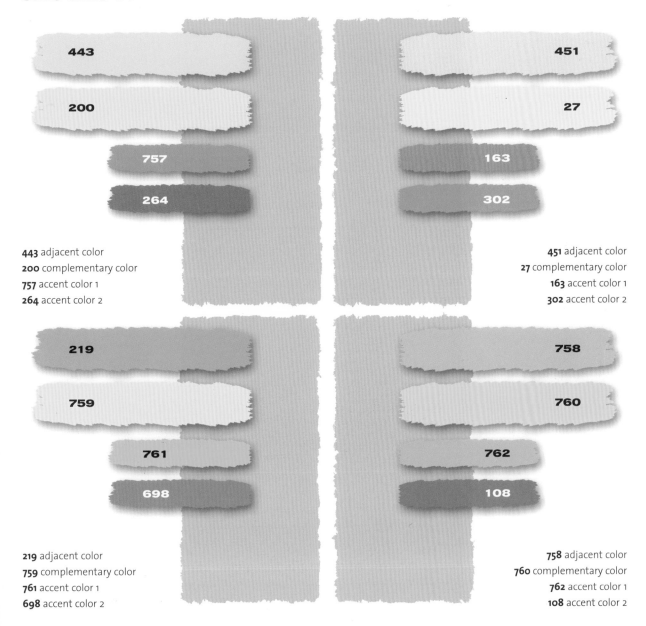

443 adjacent color
200 complementary color
757 accent color 1
264 accent color 2

451 adjacent color
27 complementary color
163 accent color 1
302 accent color 2

219 adjacent color
759 complementary color
761 accent color 1
698 accent color 2

758 adjacent color
760 complementary color
762 accent color 1
108 accent color 2

24	302
163	27

20	175
663	665

ABOVE The tones of the colors used here work perfectly together in creating a bathing space that is peaceful, but that will help you to feel refreshed and ready for the day ahead.

RIGHT Here the strong sand-colored walls and contrasting white provide balance so that the large patterned sofa does not overpower the room.

20	339
175	21

RIGHT Strong contrasts such as blue and yellow work well, particularly if one is used for accents such as pillows. This scheme is kept from being overpowering by the soft warm wall, which breaks up the intensity of the stronger contrasting tones.

20	662
443	871

LEFT The combination of cream, white and yellow offset the black work surface and give this room a fresh quality and a golden glow making it a pleasant space to spend time.

21	471
368	175

RIGHT By varying the tones of blue from light to dark and by adding touches of contrast, as in the full bowl of fruit, this cool kitchen is brought to life.

buttered yam 25

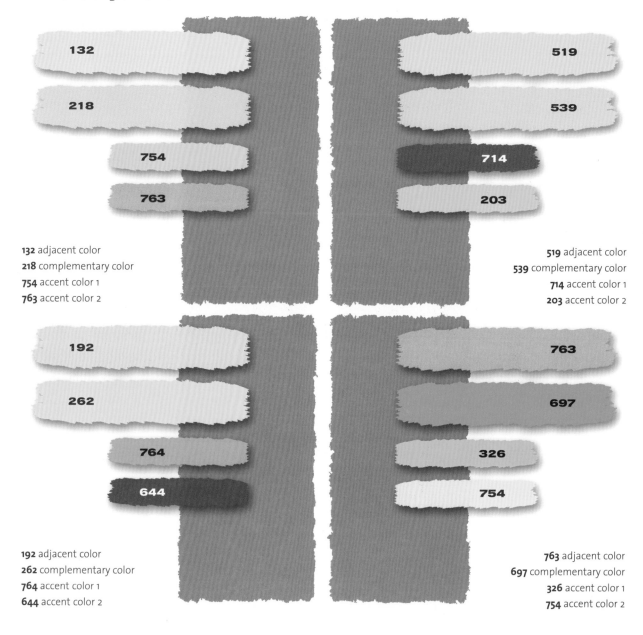

132 adjacent color
218 complementary color
754 accent color 1
763 accent color 2

519 adjacent color
539 complementary color
714 accent color 1
203 accent color 2

192 adjacent color
262 complementary color
764 accent color 1
644 accent color 2

763 adjacent color
697 complementary color
326 accent color 1
754 accent color 2

buttered yam 25

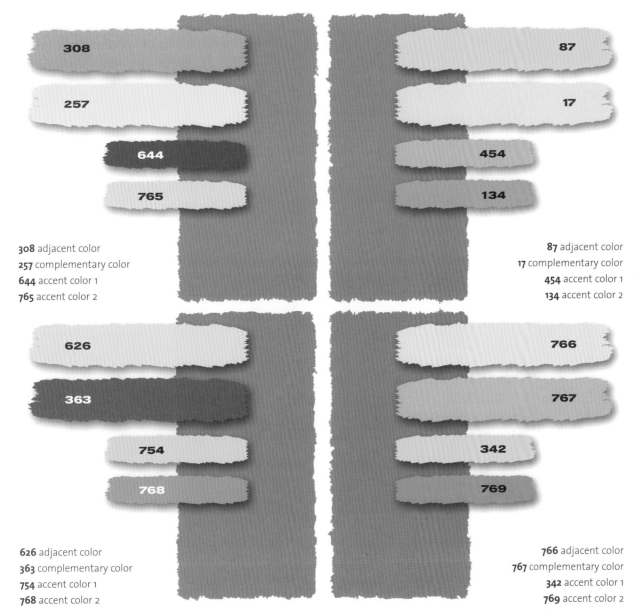

308 adjacent color
257 complementary color
644 accent color 1
765 accent color 2

87 adjacent color
17 complementary color
454 accent color 1
134 accent color 2

626 adjacent color
363 complementary color
754 accent color 1
768 accent color 2

766 adjacent color
767 complementary color
342 accent color 1
769 accent color 2

buttered yam 25

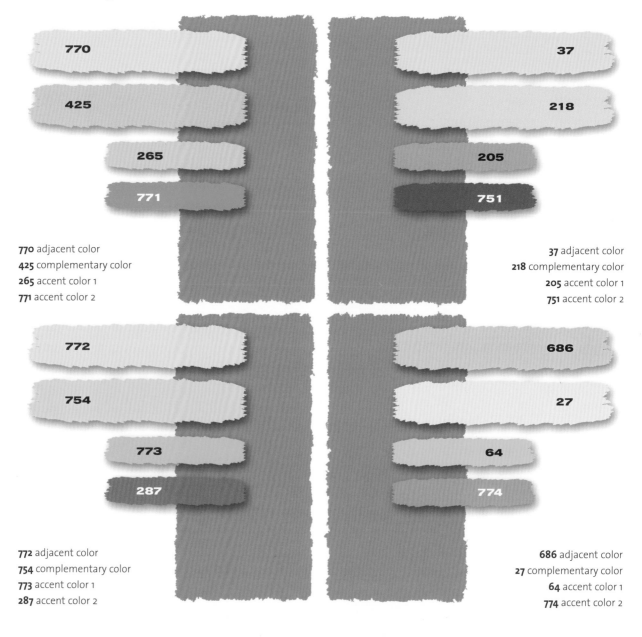

770 adjacent color
425 complementary color
265 accent color 1
771 accent color 2

37 adjacent color
218 complementary color
205 accent color 1
751 accent color 2

772 adjacent color
754 complementary color
773 accent color 1
287 accent color 2

686 adjacent color
27 complementary color
64 accent color 1
774 accent color 2

sailor's delight 26

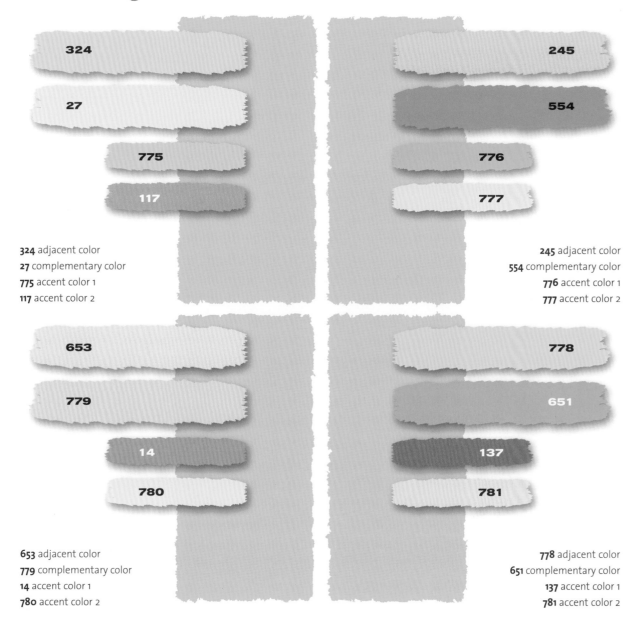

324
27
775
117

245
554
776
777

653
779
14
780

778
651
137
781

324 adjacent color
27 complementary color
775 accent color 1
117 accent color 2

245 adjacent color
554 complementary color
776 accent color 1
777 accent color 2

653 adjacent color
779 complementary color
14 accent color 1
780 accent color 2

778 adjacent color
651 complementary color
137 accent color 1
781 accent color 2

sailor's delight 26

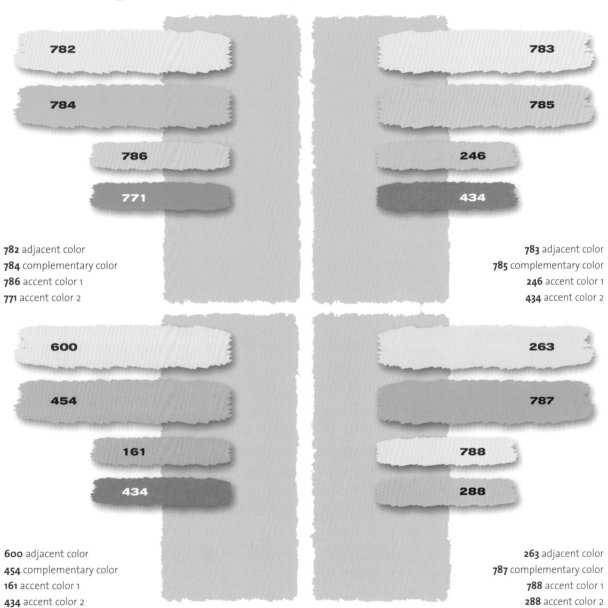

782
784
786
771

783
785
246
434

782 adjacent color
784 complementary color
786 accent color 1
771 accent color 2

783 adjacent color
785 complementary color
246 accent color 1
434 accent color 2

600
454
161
434

263
787
788
288

600 adjacent color
454 complementary color
161 accent color 1
434 accent color 2

263 adjacent color
787 complementary color
788 accent color 1
288 accent color 2

sailor's delight 26

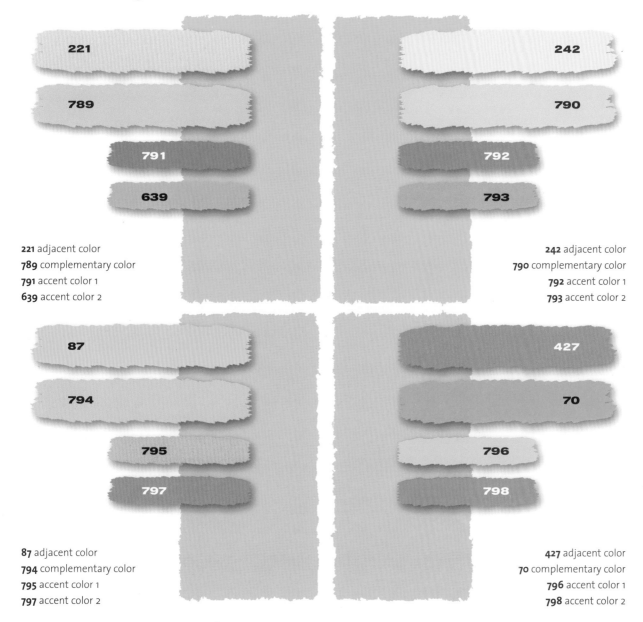

221 adjacent color
789 complementary color
791 accent color 1
639 accent color 2

242 adjacent color
790 complementary color
792 accent color 1
793 accent color 2

87 adjacent color
794 complementary color
795 accent color 1
797 accent color 2

427 adjacent color
70 complementary color
796 accent color 1
798 accent color 2

old straw hat 27

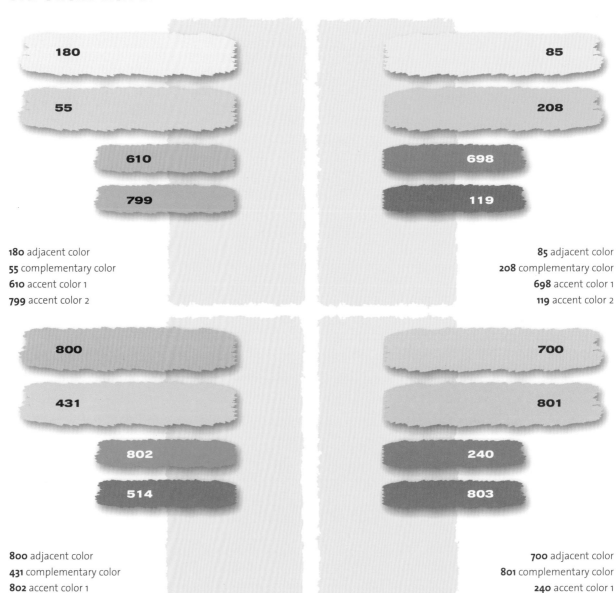

180 adjacent color
55 complementary color
610 accent color 1
799 accent color 2

85 adjacent color
208 complementary color
698 accent color 1
119 accent color 2

800 adjacent color
431 complementary color
802 accent color 1
514 accent color 2

700 adjacent color
801 complementary color
240 accent color 1
803 accent color 2

old straw hat 27

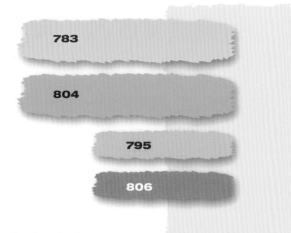

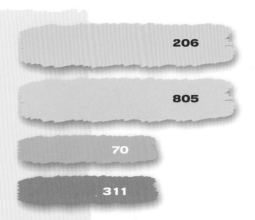

783 adjacent color
804 complementary color
795 accent color 1
806 accent color 2

206 adjacent color
805 complementary color
70 accent color 1
311 accent color 2

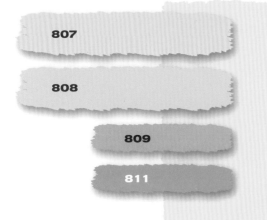

807 adjacent color
808 complementary color
809 accent color 1
811 accent color 2

158 adjacent color
222 complementary color
810 accent color 1
340 accent color 2

old straw hat 27

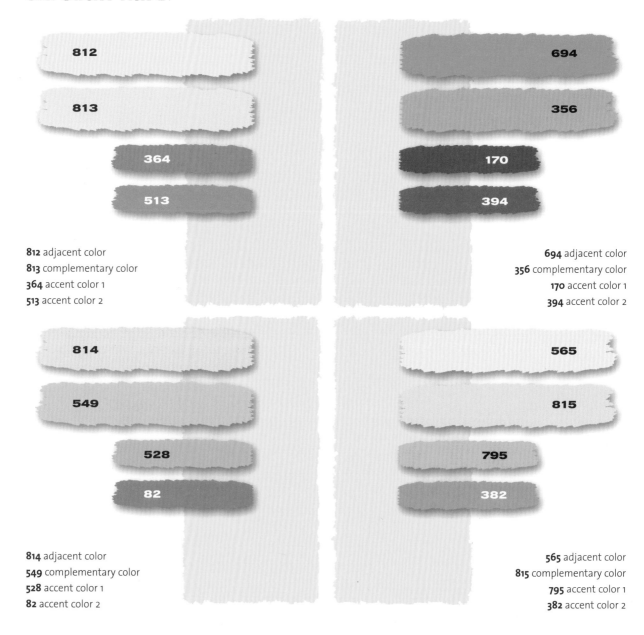

812 adjacent color
813 complementary color
364 accent color 1
513 accent color 2

694 adjacent color
356 complementary color
170 accent color 1
394 accent color 2

814 adjacent color
549 complementary color
528 accent color 1
82 accent color 2

565 adjacent color
815 complementary color
795 accent color 1
382 accent color 2

hushed hue 28

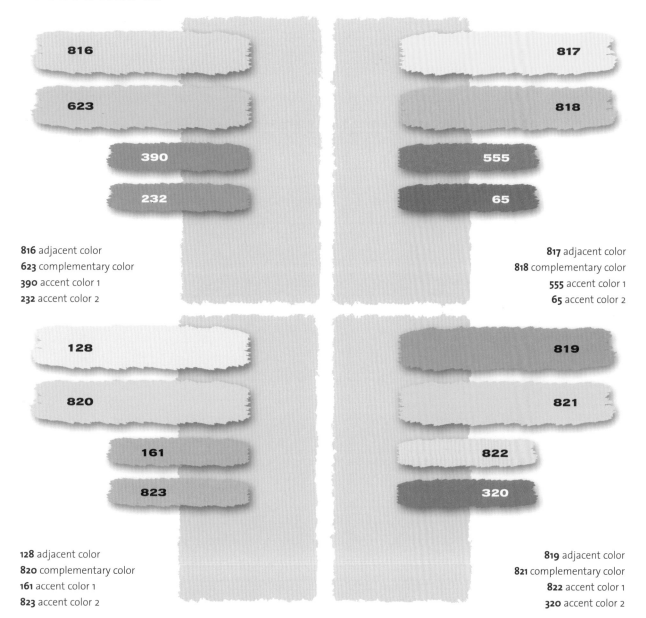

816 adjacent color
623 complementary color
390 accent color 1
232 accent color 2

817 adjacent color
818 complementary color
555 accent color 1
65 accent color 2

128 adjacent color
820 complementary color
161 accent color 1
823 accent color 2

819 adjacent color
821 complementary color
822 accent color 1
320 accent color 2

hushed hue 28

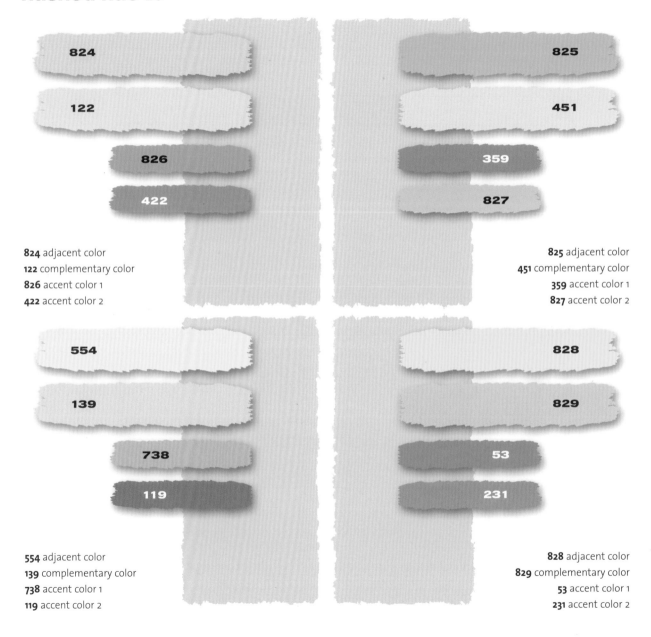

824
122
826
422

825
451
359
827

824 adjacent color
122 complementary color
826 accent color 1
422 accent color 2

825 adjacent color
451 complementary color
359 accent color 1
827 accent color 2

554
139
738
119

828
829
53
231

554 adjacent color
139 complementary color
738 accent color 1
119 accent color 2

828 adjacent color
829 complementary color
53 accent color 1
231 accent color 2

hushed hue 28

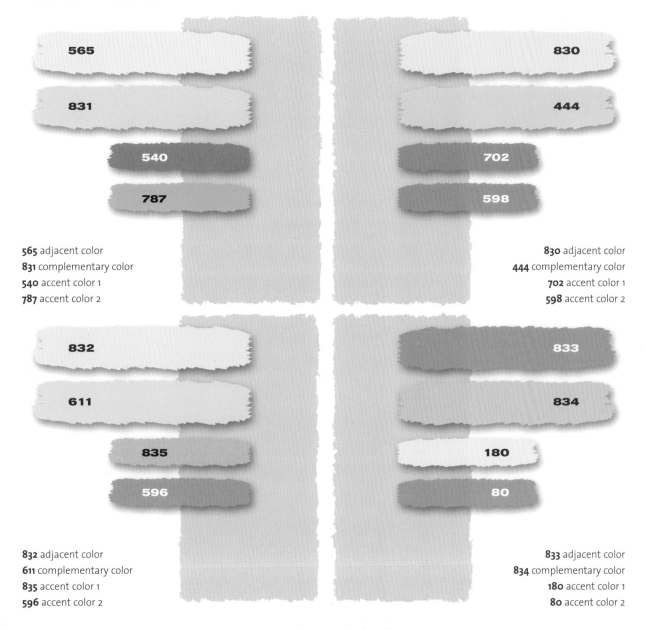

565 adjacent color
831 complementary color
540 accent color 1
787 accent color 2

830 adjacent color
444 complementary color
702 accent color 1
598 accent color 2

832 adjacent color
611 complementary color
835 accent color 1
596 accent color 2

833 adjacent color
834 complementary color
180 accent color 1
80 accent color 2

crisp morning air 29

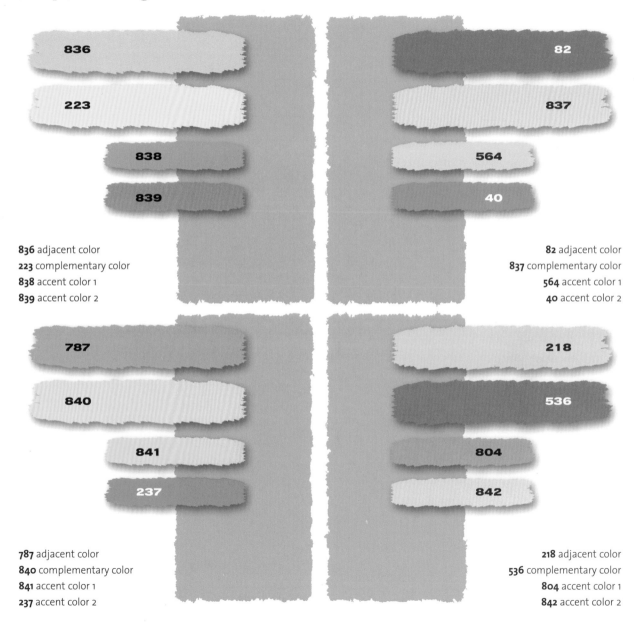

836 adjacent color
223 complementary color
838 accent color 1
839 accent color 2

82 adjacent color
837 complementary color
564 accent color 1
40 accent color 2

787 adjacent color
840 complementary color
841 accent color 1
237 accent color 2

218 adjacent color
536 complementary color
804 accent color 1
842 accent color 2

crisp morning air 29

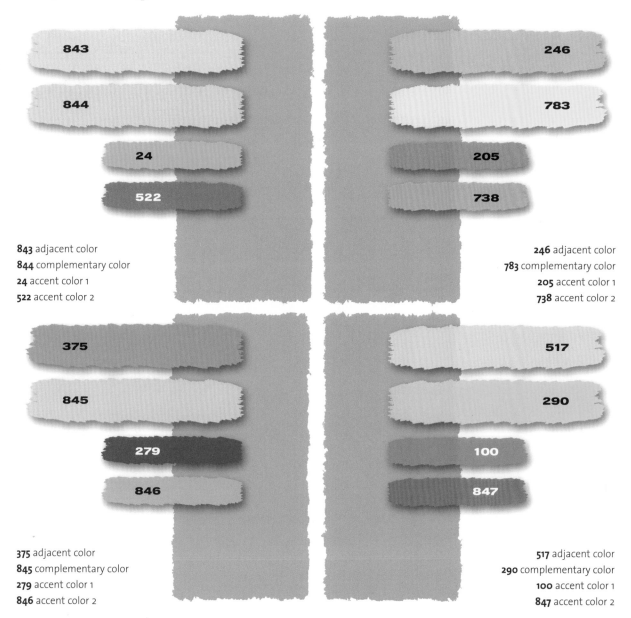

843 adjacent color
844 complementary color
24 accent color 1
522 accent color 2

246 adjacent color
783 complementary color
205 accent color 1
738 accent color 2

375 adjacent color
845 complementary color
279 accent color 1
846 accent color 2

517 adjacent color
290 complementary color
100 accent color 1
847 accent color 2

crisp morning air 29

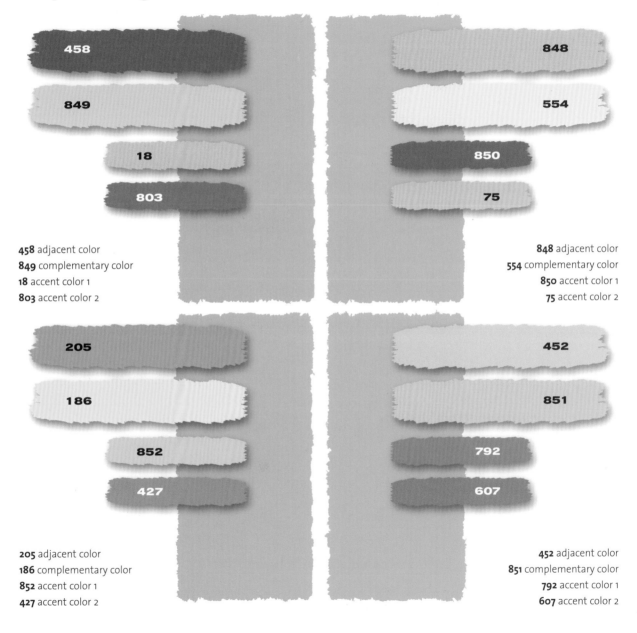

458

849

18

803

848

554

850

75

458 adjacent color
849 complementary color
18 accent color 1
803 accent color 2

848 adjacent color
554 complementary color
850 accent color 1
75 accent color 2

205

186

852

427

452

851

792

607

205 adjacent color
186 complementary color
852 accent color 1
427 accent color 2

452 adjacent color
851 complementary color
792 accent color 1
607 accent color 2

mint julep 30

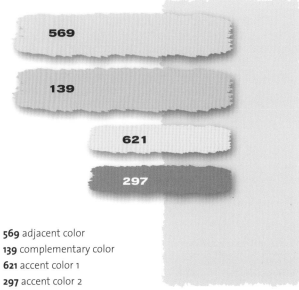

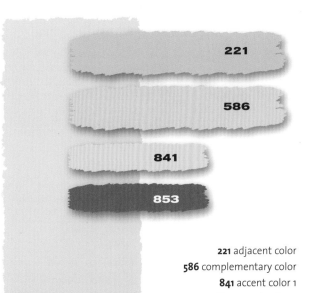

569 adjacent color
139 complementary color
621 accent color 1
297 accent color 2

221 adjacent color
586 complementary color
841 accent color 1
853 accent color 2

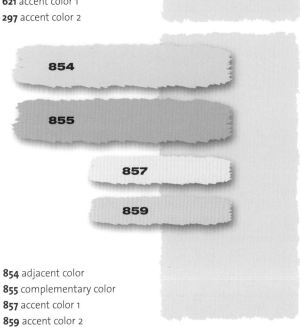

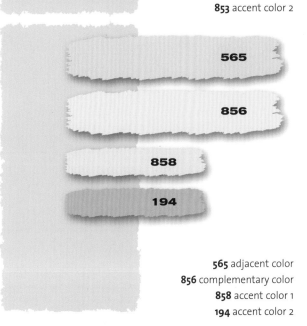

854 adjacent color
855 complementary color
857 accent color 1
859 accent color 2

565 adjacent color
856 complementary color
858 accent color 1
194 accent color 2

mint julep 30

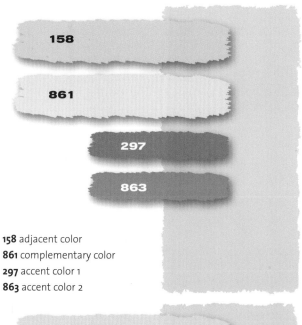

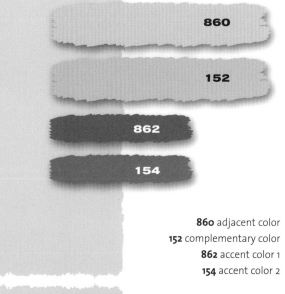

158 adjacent color
861 complementary color
297 accent color 1
863 accent color 2

860 adjacent color
152 complementary color
862 accent color 1
154 accent color 2

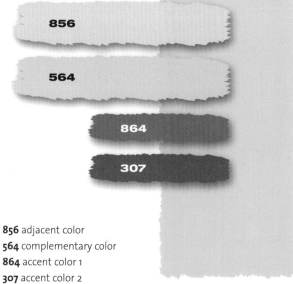

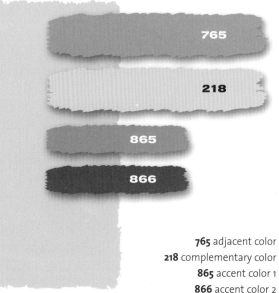

856 adjacent color
564 complementary color
864 accent color 1
307 accent color 2

765 adjacent color
218 complementary color
865 accent color 1
866 accent color 2

mint julep 30

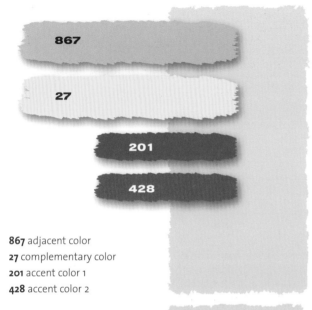

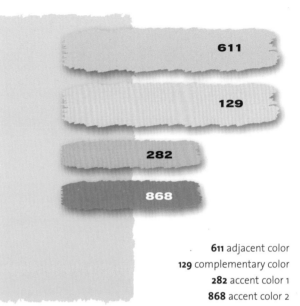

867 adjacent color
27 complementary color
201 accent color 1
428 accent color 2

611 adjacent color
129 complementary color
282 accent color 1
868 accent color 2

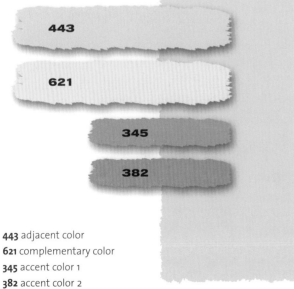

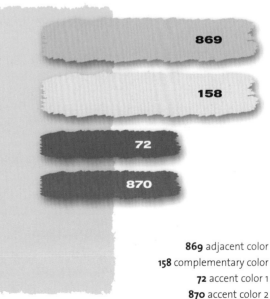

443 adjacent color
621 complementary color
345 accent color 1
382 accent color 2

869 adjacent color
158 complementary color
72 accent color 1
870 accent color 2

25	714
221	3

780	791
519	639

ABOVE Providing the perfect place to relax, this is a classic combination of red and white. The assuredness of these contrasts is underlined by the classic materials on offer: leather, glass, wood, stone, and terracotta.

RIGHT Blue, green and yellow are a combination of colors often found in nature, that can be used to create a relaxed, simple, and fresh kitchen that is a cheerful and social place to spend time in, and that has a timeless quality.

28	528
170	871

RIGHT The neutral color of the walls in combination with warm tan, with a hint of pink and lilac, generate an air of sophistication and calm in this bedroom.

28	26
158	871

LEFT A color scheme chosen to work with the view, the pink sofa is complementary to the blue sky whilst the gray walls provide the perfect backdrop to the sofa.

25	519
714	203

RIGHT The use of neutral textures and materials works well together with the strong focal point of the fireplace to enhance the sense of harmony and relaxation.

color index

BM No. These refer to the numbering system in the Benjamin Moore Classic and Affinity ranges.

Swatch	Code	BM No.	CMYK	Swatch	Code	BM No.	CMYK	Swatch	Code	BM No.	CMYK
	1	1357	30c 71m 34y 34k		56	901	2c 11m 18y		115	625	29c 3m 25y
	2	1272	13c 56m 25y 3k		57	1496	38c 30m 45y 11k		116	1540	45c 46m 57y 34k
	3	1467	32c 24m 27y 4k		58	1274	25c 77m 61y 22k		117	377	10c 31m 68y 2k
	4	1105	17c 51m 64y 6k		59	878	7c 12m 11y		118	1679	83c 26m 28y 22k
	5	793	38c 11m 11y		60	1276	4c 29m 12y		119	433	43c 26m 67y 19k
	6	673	30c 3m 19y		61	872	10c 4m 10y		120	1269	1c 26m 10y
	7	1372	48c 64m 20y 27k		62	1370	25c 45m 10y 4k		121	1455	48c 43m 38y 24k
	8	1196	22c 69m 69y 14k		63	2	31m 23y		122	1492	12c 7m 15y
	9	1262	11c 22m 13y		64	180	28m 58y		123	1658	75c 21m 32y 14k
	10	1144	6c 31m 39y 1k		65	706	58c 25m 44y 18k		124	1280	20c 62m 39y 9k
	11	1432	44c 18m 10y 2k		66	822	50c 14m 11y 2k		125	123	32m 49y
	12	af710	45c 34m 38y 15k		67	194	8c 40m 61y 1k		126	1476	40c 37m 45y 16k
	13	af385	17c 24m 42y 3k		68	224	23c 49m 77y 16k		127	723	43c 1m 19y
	14	47	14c 57m 49y 4k		69	111	6c 55m 64y 1k		128	925	6c 6m 16y
	15	1011	19c 28m 28y 2k		70	301	44m 82y		129	232	7c 12m 20y
	16	1411	30c 18m 12y 1k		71	716	31c 5m 17y		130	708	28c 6m 21y
	17	414	10c 2m 30y		72	259	23c 49m 82y 17k		131	1639	28c 6m 16y
	18	1437	26c 11m 13y 1k		73	1021	34c 49m 54y 24k		132	332	1c 9m 35y
	19	af285	14c 75m 64y 3k		74	359	1c 11m 43y		133	1490	46c 44m 56y 32k
	20	343	32m 92y		75	381	12c 16m 39y 1k		134	425	35c 6m 59y 2k
	21	796	78c 8m 13y 1k		76	1288	23c 80m 68y 14k		135	1670	60c 17m 25y 8k
	22	1091	19c 55m 69y 9k		77	1347	3c 62m 4y		136	1240	9c 17m 14y
	23	339	1c 12m 47y		78	1350	19c 84m 50y 6k		137	248	10c 21m 38y 1k
	24	396	10c 14m 65y 1k		79	1517	26c 26m 41y 5k		138	1437	26c 11m 13y 1k
	25	af230	8c 65m 82y 1k		80	1390	33c 38m 6y 2k		139	401	11c 5m 40y
	26	1296	34m 18y		81	1249	19c 28m 19y 2k		140	1292	7c 50m 31y 1k
	27	337	1c 7m 27y		82	1420	62c 34m 9y 6k		141	245	31c 43m 56y 17k
	28	1520	12c 12m 20y		83	1203	21c 74m 66y 10k		142	1440	52c 34m 24y 13k
	29	780	51c 12y		84	132	41m 60y		143	440	44c 26m 57y 15k
	30	547	16c 1m 25y		85	211	3c 8m 22y		144	491	13c 9m 23y
	31	1252	39c 53m 41y 26k		86	1296	34m 18y		145	204	4c 8m 20y
	32	1363	21c 59m 13y 5k		87	171	21m 48y		146	435	18c 7m 23y
	33	948	5c 12m 21y		88	1342	16c 76m 43y 5k		147	715	20c 3m 14y
	34	684	63c 20m 45y 15k		89	af625	31c 54m 26y 16k		148	510	40c 37m 57y 20k
	35	828	38c 10m 12y 1k		90	af495	51c 19m 37y 9k		149	376	9c 25m 54y 1k
	36	4	50m 42y		91	1371	37c 60m 18y 16k		150	628	53c 17m 50y 11k
	37	333	1c 13m 48y		92	356	25m 81y		151	1478	16c 8m 15y
	38	1676	49c 7m 18y 2k		93	1382	23c 22m 9y 1k		152	1444	19c 17m 15y 1k
	39	1392	52c 59m 16y 20k		94	175	1c 48m 81y		153	680	21c 1m 18y
	40	1200	8c 49m 39y 1k		95	af240	25c 70m 85y 27k		154	1448	40c 43m 32y 15k
	41	835	37c 5m 14y 1k		96	af75	15c 8m 21y		155	1622	55c 26m 30y 12k
	42	701	28c 8m 21y 1k		97	1559	39c 31m 38y 10k		156	1588	54c 33m 39y 19k
	43	1355	14c 59m 13y 3k		98	af185	18c 35m 35y 4k		157	344	2c 8m 22y
	44	218	3c 11m 23y		99	af255	2c 7m 9y		158	393	6c 5m 29y
	45	839	70c 22m 24y 13k		100	1377	25c 43m 12y 4k		159	407	12c 2m 27y
	46	1367	6c 19m 6y		101	1290	2c 28m 16y		160	596	23c 1m 19y
	47	1544	32c 34m 38y 9k		102	349	29m 79y		161	382	10c 26m 52y 2k
	48	626	37c 4m 33y 1k		103	691	60c 22m 42y 17k		162	518	43c 44m 64y 33k
	49	579	63c 50y		104	357	1c 30m 90y		163	405	27c 22m 79y 10k
	50	1566	48c 28m 37y 12k		105	119	5c 61m 75y 1k		164	719	62c 19m 33y 11k
	51	1606	42c 26m 28y 7k		106	315	41m 82y		165	859	19c 16m 22y 1k
	52	634	52c 15m 43y 8k		107	1653	30c 2m 14y		166	1458	17c 12m 15y
	53	1447	35c 37m 28y 9k		108	251	2c 45m 72y 14k		167	865	15c 4m 14y
	54	1320	65m 43y		109	1236	29c 53m 52y 23k		168	1481	31c 18m 26y 2k
	55	867	24c 5m 16y		110	283	1c 10m 33y		169	1095	12c 22m 33y 1k
					111	35	22c 76m 74y 12k		170	1449	41c 54m 43y 30k
					112	22	2c 14m 17y		171	1454	40c 38m 31y 11k
					113	323	1c 8m 29y		172	1484	56c 44m 52y 43k
					114	1674	29c 3m 13y		173	1513	9c 7m 16y

Swatch	Code	BM No.	CMYK	Swatch	Code	BM No.	CMYK	Swatch	Code	BM No.	CMYK
	174	687	32c 8m 21y 1k		233	162	2c 11m 25y		292	1316	21c 85m 69y 9k
	175	48	24c 66m 56y 19k		234	29	2c 18m 16y		293	1368	11c 26m 5y
	176	1489	44c 42m 54y 26k		235	326	16m 59y		294	41	18c 68m 64y 7k
	177	489	4c 35m 67y 26k		236	1435	65c 41m 30y 30k		295	317	11m 38y
	178	1456	51c 49m 44y 35k		237	1216	11c 47m 47y 2k		296	199	1c 21m 39y
	179	1563	27c 12m 22y 1k		238	676	56c 5m 31y 1k		297	530	29c 29m 68y 12k
	180	932	4c 5m 17y		239	802	70c 9m 19y 2k		298	33	5c 67m 57y 1k
	181	1646	21c 4m 14y		240	1098	19c 44m 62y 9k		299	1307	8c 84m 76y 1k
	182	941	11c 14m 26y		241	929	3c 9m 23y		300	1326	44m 13y
	183	474	41c 29m 48y 13k		242	330	2c 6m 21y		301	1364	26c 72m 27y 23k
	184	193	4c 31m 48y 1k		243	1000	41c 49m 59y 35k		302	294	6c 46m 84y 1k
	185	244	27c 36m 50y 10k		244	231	32c 49m 73y 30k		303	271	15c 33m 52y 4k
	186	148	1c 12m 25y		245	369	4c 20m 56y 1k		304	280	21c 44m 76y 13k
	187	8	1c 21m 17y		246	411	21c 5m 56y 1k		305	1386	54c 65m 23y 43k
	188	506	21c 12m 24y 1k		247	1555	15c 10m 18y		306	1398	51c 49m 3y 2k
	189	1002	12c 15m 18y		248	885	3c 13m 10y		307	797	98c 25m 14y 13k
	190	1190	24c 72m 72y 17k		249	1012	25c 37m 38y 8k		308	364	8c 31m 92y 1k
	191	675	46c 3m 26y 1k		250	1560	42c 35m 45y 16k		309	1360	6c 24m 7y
	192	78	1c 16m 18y		251	1013	31c 47m 49y 18k		310	68	1c 45m 48y
	193	1416	25c 7m 8y		252	1015	33c 56m 57y 32k		311	783	95c 7m 23y 1k
	194	403	16c 11m 66y 2k		253	818	85c 28m 9y 7k		312	196	18c 53m 79y 9k
	195	1504	40c 38m 55y 20k		254	15	1c 18m 16y		313	77	16c 79m 84y 5k
	196	1657	67c 15m 26y 7k		255	138	38m 49y		314	105	23c 69m 81y 15k
	197	782	82c 1m 20y		256	832	72c 37m 23y 26k		315	396	10c 14m 65y 1k
	198	415	12c 3m 38y		257	345	1c 9m 28y		316	308	1c 50m 91y
	199	930	3c 9m 27y		258	47	14c 57m 49y 4k		317	14	1c 74m 73y
	200	57	1c 14m 19y		259	125	47m 67y		318	754	96c 11m 42y 2k
	201	517	38c 44m 65y 28k		260	419	42c 7m 88y 1k		319	46	6c 45m 35y 1k
	202	539	37c 29m 72y 18k		261	481	32c 23m 47y 6k		320	831	63c 30m 19y 13k
	203	348	21m 65y		262	352	1c 11m 42y		321	536	22c 11m 41y 1k
	204	131	35m 52y		263	408	13c 2m 33y		322	325	1c 12m 45y
	205	412	34c 11m 75y 4k		264	516	30c 40m 60y 16k		323	76	4c 71m 77y 1k
	206	305	22m 46y		265	292	1c 25m 59y		324	1	21m 17y
	207	934	4c 7m 23y		266	103	4c 50m 55y 1k		325	166	1c 35m 55y
	208	410	18c 4m 47y 1k		267	663	80c 43y		326	342	27m 82y
	209	1663	56c 12m 22y 4k		268	1396	32c 28m 1y 1k		327	488	37c 27m 60y 13k
	210	378	15c 40m 79y 6k		269	690	52c 18m 37y 9k		328	260	3c 10m 25y
	211	1583	21c 8m 18y		270	1548	13c 10m 17y		329	756	97c 26m 47y 24k
	212	848	21c 1m 16y		271	526	12c 10m 31y		330	915	3c 11m 21y
	213	1037	12c 17m 24y 1k		272	726	85c 14m 41y 4k		331	1372	48c 64m 20y 27k
	214	281	3c 7m 21y		273	1553	39c 38m 46y 16k		332	327	20m 71y
	215	1594	50c 32m 36y 15k		274	1677	62c 15m 22y 7k		333	1358	39c 64m 46y 43k
	216	677	71c 15m 42y 7k		275	1412	42c 25m 15y 4k		334	1163	5c 18m 18y
	217	1488	38c 34m 45y 13k		276	1536	28c 24m 32y 4k		335	274	2c 14m 35y
	218	409	15c 3m 36y		277	808	49c 8m 14y 1k		336	1391	41c 50m 9y 5k
	219	605	53c 33y		278	253	4c 11m 25y		337	1405	47c 34m 8y 4k
	220	358	1c 9m 36y		279	1427	63c 40m 24y 23k		338	1330	21c 84m 64y 10k
	221	512	9c 12m 23y		280	1258	21c 44m 76y 13k		339	1339	1c 37m 10y
	222	432	37c 19m 59y 9k		281	af590	50c 42m 31y 20k		340	406	33c 24m 82y 15k
	223	365	1c 9m 28y		282	215	5c 27m 54y 1k		341	21	69m 75y
	224	623	87c 24m 63y 22k		283	360	1c 14m 55y		342	361	16m 64y
	225	1649	60c 23m 29y 12k		284	7	80m 86y		343	765	37c 14y
	226	1516	20c 19m 31y 1k		285	1312	58m 29y		344	1272	13c 56m 25y 3k
	227	36	3c 22m 17y		286	28	5c 72m 70y 1k		345	228	15c 30m 47y 4k
	228	351	1c 8m 30y		287	34	16c 75m 71y 5k		346	840	76c 39m 29y 36k
	229	1518	31c 36m 53y 13k		288	336	26m 89y		347	247	7c 16m 30y
	230	1048	21c 48m 67y 12k		289	322	37m 93y		348	321	35m 90y
	231	1419	54c 26m 9y 4k		290	1303	30m 18y		349	19	51m 49y
	232	431	34c 17m 53y 6k		291	1233	18c 30m 28y 3k		350	1375	18c 25m 10y 1k

Swatch	Code	BM No.	CMYK	Swatch	Code	BM No.	CMYK	Swatch	Code	BM No.	CMYK
	351	747	72c 5m 30y 1k		410	af705	46c 36m 36y 16k		469	1591	24c 12m 19y 1k
	352	309	2c 9m 25y		411	af550	54c 27m 27y 11k		470	1221	17c 54m 60y 6k
	353	1399	66c 59m 11y 13k		412	af565	66c 47m 37y 45k		471	1421	83c 53m 14y 17k
	354	742	98c 23m 53y 14k		413	af560	61c 43m 41y 36k		472	1428	63c 51m 34y 44k
	355	229	18c 37m 57y 7k		414	af645	50c 58m 40y 44k		473	af330	1c 9m 29y
	356	1438	36c 19m 15y 2k		415	af530	87c 31m 26y 30k		474	af205	6c 37m 39y 1k
	357	1445	26c 22m 19y 1k		416	af630	40c 63m 31y 33k		475	af570	47c 27m 22y 7k
	358	337	1c 7m 27y		417	492	15c 13m 28y 1k		476	af460	45c 31m 49y 16k
	359	1208	72c 56m 54y 5k		418	1064	23c 56m 77y 20k		477	af355	19c 51m 68y 9k
	360	1383	35c 36m 15y 6k		419	836	43c 7m 16y 1k		478	af270	22c 60m 45y 13k
	361	461	51c 32m 53y 24k		420	630	63c 30m 63y 41k		479	af160	31c 50m 53y 22k
	362	1470	46c 46m 49y 29k		421	1575	55c 39m 50y 32k		480	af170	42c 55m 57y 42k
	363	1218	23c 66m 73y 16k		422	1524	27c 33m 48y 9k		481	af355	19c 51m 68y 9k
	364	1194	14c 55m 50y 4k		423	1547	52c 48m 54y 44k		482	af215	11c 47m 51y 2k
	365	437	23c 8m 28y 1k		424	573	67c 8m 72y 2k		483	af595	32c 36m 18y 5k
	366	1619	27c 9m 15y		425	527	15c 14m 39y 1k		484	af545	41c 20m 22y 4k
	367	1616	57c 42m 41y 32k		426	543	34c 16m 58y 6k		485	af125	22c 41m 49y 9k
	368	1131	18c 48m 58y 8k		427	515	25c 31m 48y 7k		486	af635	43c 49m 33y 22k
	369	717	43c 8m 23y 2k		428	546	50c 25m 72y 27k		487	af155	34c 35m 41y 10k
	370	633	45c 10m 35y 4k		429	679	77c 31m 45y 42k		488	af85	8c 14m 23y
	371	1434	60c 34m 26y 17k		430	225	6c 11m 21y		489	af245	16c 38m 40y 4k
	372	168	10c 62m 87y 2k		431	583	28c 23y		490	af615	22c 27m 16y 2k
	373	269	8c 17m 30y		432	823	59c 20m 13y 5k		491	af585	40c 30m 22y 7k
	374	1472	25c 17m 22y 1k		433	483	40c 36m 64y 23k		492	af105	31c 41m 54y 16k
	375	1424	41c 19m 12y 2k		434	385	21c 38m 81y 12k		493	af640	45c 47m 37y 24k
	376	217	13c 48m 80y 4k		435	622	76c 13m 59y 5k		494	af40	4c 8m 13y
	377	1439	44c 25m 19y 5k		436	720	74c 26m 38y 25k		495	af345	9c 30m 50y 2k
	378	900	3c 9m 17y		437	528	16c 16m 43y 1k		496	af600	40c 41m 23y 11k
	379	1139	17c 51m 62y 6k		438	800	49c 2m 31y		497	af395	31c 30m 42y 8k
	380	1384	41c 43m 16y 9k		439	448	60c 38m 56y 41k		498	af475	54c 29m 49y 21k
	381	1566	48c 28m 37y 12k		440	825	75c 35m 17y 21k		499	af305	3c 8m 21y
	382	426	39c 9m 66y 3k		441	935	8c 6m 17y		500	af280	16c 78m 78y 5k
	383	389	7c 17m 46y 1k		442	858	15c 13m 19y		501	af525	82c 23m 30y 16k
	384	1225	27c 81m 64y 31k		443	624	20c 1m 19y		502	af165	32c 57m 66y 36k
	385	542	29c 11m 45y 2k		444	834	32c 3m 13y		503	af335	3c 21m 35y
	386	1621	45c 19m 23y 5k		445	1581	54c 38m 46y 28k		504	af620	30c 30m 21y 4k
	387	629	62c 23m 59y 24k		446	476	51c 41m 62y 37k		505	af675	36c 30m 29y 6k
	388	290	1c 18m 45y		447	1666	80c 36m 43y 43k		506	af295	25c 86m 69y 17k
	389	238	35c 48m 66y 30k		448	494	26c 24m 46y 5k		507	85	2c 12m 18y
	390	40	10c 59m 49y 2k		449	416	17c 5m 54y 1k		508	477	14c 9m 27y
	391	471	25c 12m 28y 1k		450	421	14c 1m 26y		509	1224	26c 60m 62y 25k
	392	1301	23c 81m 76y 15k		451	533	12c 5m 23y		510	1267	29c 70m 56y 45k
	393	1257	26c 57m 42y 19k		452	575	32c 24y		511	1275	3c 20m 11y
	394	1441	58c 40m 29y 23k		453	736	37c 18y		512	1369	14c 34m 5y 1k
	395	1629	59c 31m 28y 16k		454	397	9c 16m 79y 2k		513	1264	20c 42m 27y 6k
	396	1680	82c 38m 32y 42k		455	241	16c 22m 34y 2k		514	1426	58c 34m 19y 14k
	397	1154	14c 47m 52y 4k		456	239	10c 15m 25y		515	71	1c 20m 22y
	398	1404	36c 27m 8y 2k		457	423	22c 2m 38y		516	1352	4c 19m 9y
	399	444	37c 15m 38y 4k		458	770	98c 23m 36y 14k		517	1394	14c 11m 5y
	400	1232	37c 60m 58y 42k		459	373	3c 10m 29y		518	1379	43c 64m 27y 35k
	401	279	11c 40m 77y 3k		460	980	43c 45m 53y 29k		519	916	1c 15m 26y
	402	1400	69c 63m 13y 16k		461	420	54c 11m 96y 3k		520	246	5c 10m 23y
	403	475	46c 35m 55y 22k		462	1430	29c 11m 8y 1k		521	966	15c 20m 28y 1k
	404	210	13c 46m 76y 3k		463	1457	13c 10m 14y		522	384	20c 36m 73y 10k
	405	242	18c 23m 37y 2k		464	890	5c 6m 12y		523	9	1c 27m 19y
	406	1648	48c 15m 22y 4k		465	868	23c 7m 15y		524	537	25c 18m 52y 4k
	407	529	21c 21m 54y 4k		466	1001	44c 51m 60y 40k		525	1407	74c 60m 14y 19k
	408	804	95c 24m 20y 17k		467	1510	31c 28m 44y 7k		526	1359	4c 17m 9y
	409	af405	35c 27m 51y 10k		468	1403	27c 17m 7y 1k		527	1212	2c 14m 16y

Swatch	Code	BM No.	CMYK	Swatch	Code	BM No.	CMYK	Swatch	Code	BM No.	CMYK
	528	1389	23c 27m 6y 1k		587	439	35c 19m 45y 6k		646	1378	39c 56m 20y 18k
	529	1334	50m 24y		588	1281	26c 71m 54y 21k		647	340	17c 62y
	530	1413	52c 38m 25y 15k		589	697	43c 20m 37y 7k		648	1270	5c 36m 11y 1k
	531	1406	55c 42m 9y 6k		590	1494	25c 18m 29y 2k		649	1289	3c 20m 14y
	532	1009	10c 16m 17y		591	1660	24c 2m 13y		650	203	10c 49m 87y 2k
	533	1338	2c 20m 10y		592	417	25c 6m 68y 1k		651	154	48m 73y
	534	1423	29c 14m 13y 1k		593	1538	39c 38m 47y 16k		652	1311	38m 13y
	535	1431	34c 13m 7y 1k		594	1331	2c 18m 11y		653	1065	6c 12m 21y
	536	1228	19c 49m 50y 8k		595	1511	34c 36m 51y 14k		654	81	41m 44y
	537	1665	79c 27m 32y 24k		596	1425	48c 24m 16y 5k		655	1305	67m 54y
	538	960	10c 9m 16y		597	806	30c 3m 11y		656	1300	20c 81m 77y 9k
	539	1415	20c 8m 6y		598	838	59c 18m 20y 7k		657	1192	3c 29m 22y 1k
	540	978	34c 38m 47y 13k		599	1090	15c 45m 54y 5k		658	1344	25c 83m 55y 17k
	541	1512	39c 42m 59y 24k		600	379	6c 10m 27y		659	1335	68m 42y
	542	1463	47c 52m 52y 41k		601	1565	41c 20m 29y 5k		660	1155	21c 59m 67y 12k
	543	1385	50c 52m 19y 20k		602	1265	27c 57m 39y 19k		661	133	55m 77y
	544	1443	12c 11m 10y		603	550	42c 3m 57y 1k		662	346	1c 11m 39y
	545	1093	7c 15m 22y		604	619	40 1m 27y 1k		663	27	2c 63m 57y
	546	799	39c 2m 12y		605	554	16c 1m 29y		664	80	25m 25y
	547	1671	66c 23m 31y 15k		606	480	28c 17m 40y 3k		665	182	5c 50m 79y 1k
	548	230	26c 42m 64y 15k		607	503	32c 31m 60y 12k		666	1230	27c 60m 61y 28k
	549	1633	31c 8m 18y 1k		608	127	2c 10m 20y		667	1223	23c 58m 63y 16k
	550	1462	48c 42m 42y 24k		609	807	34c 3m 11y		668	1279	13c 56m 31y 3k
	551	1149	4c 15m 21y		610	514	18c 20m 35y 2k		669	1308	12c 83m 74y 2k
	552	1451	20c 14m 16y 1k		611	792	29c 1m 10y		670	147	51m 77y
	553	696	36c 14m 30y 3k		612	1634	45c 15m 25y 4k		671	41	18c 68m 64y 7k
	554	372	2c 7m 22y		613	1507	17c 12m 22y 1k		672	1128	12c 26m 32y 1k
	555	524	30c 35m 62y 14k		614	268	7c 12m 23y		673	176	2c 11m 28y
	556	441	52c 36m 65y 35k		615	1576	21c 10m 18y		674	75	1c 56m 59y
	557	143	20m 37y		616	1521	16c 15m 23y 1k		675	380	7c 14m 32y
	558	428	7c 4m 25y		617	190	3c 8m 20y		676	222	12c 35m 56y 3k
	559	522	20c 20m 39y 2k		618	1593	42c 24m 28y 6k		677	250	18c 40m 67y 8k
	560	566	68c 20m 75y 17k		619	582	21c 1m 17y		678	126	3c 60m 79y 1k
	561	1436	18c 6m 11y		620	844	9c 3m 11y		679	1329	14c 85m 61y 3k
	562	1366	7c 13m 8y		621	884	3c 11m 10y		680	1365	35c 69m 36y 40k
	563	999	37c 46m 53y 24k		622	584	36c 27y		681	1217	18c 59m 63y 7k
	564	813	23c 1m 10y		623	541	21c 7m 36y 1k		682	af540	21c 4m 11y
	565	897	3c 7m 16y		624	220	5c 20m 36y 1k		683	1604	23c 12m 17y
	566	861	24c 23m 27y 2k		625	718	50c 13m 27y 4k		684	272	17c 35m 56y 6k
	567	236	26c 41m 59y 14k		626	99	1c 16m 19y		685	1656	55c 8m 22y 2k
	568	1235	27c 50m 51y 19k		627	452	42c 19m 42y 7k		686	362	22m 79y
	569	1388	17c 18m 6y		628	109	1c 39m 47y		687	1429	24c 10m 8y
	570	911	3c 8m 17y		629	766	47c 17y		688	1374	11c 18m 11y
	571	1493	16c 11m 21y		630	1605	32c 17m 23y 2k		689	1151	8c 15m 22y
	572	1442	61c 49m 44y 50k		631	1545	40c 40m 46y 17k		690	1245	33c 54m 47y 25k
	573	561	26c 3m 31y		632	725	71c 7m 32y		691	1222	19c 58m 62y 9k
	574	1380	13c 16m 7y		633	1567	52c 32m 42y 19k		692	1402	22c 13m 7y
	575	375	5c 19m 43y 1k		634	1554	43c 47m 56y 31k		693	1202	17c 69m 64y 6k
	576	1141	25c 60m 70y 24k		635	af250	3c 15m 14y		694	1256	14c 46m 29y 3k
	577	1244	28c 46m 34y 11k		636	603	28c 19y		695	449	25c 5m 11y
	578	1401	17c 7m 7y		637	363	1c 26m 86y		696	453	46c 26m 49y 14k
	579	1227	16c 42m 42y 5k		638	586	64c 2m 52y 1k		697	371	10c 31m 85y 2k
	580	1294	19c 69m 57y 8k		639	350	1c 37m 90y		698	273	21c 39m 64y 11k
	581	1302	27c 71m 60y 33k		640	65	1c 19m 22y		699	694	26c 8m 22y 1k
	582	936	9c 7m 18y		641	61	1c 45m 47y		700	395	10c 8m 51y 1k
	583	1501	25c 19m 31y 2k		642	353	1c 16m 59y		701	277	6c 26m 57y 1k
	584	1373	7c 12m 11y		643	817	77c 18m 6y 3k		702	698	47c 21m 41y 10k
	585	1499	13c 10m 18y		644	42	26c 75m 66y 26k		703	398	11c 22m 87y 3k
	586	722	35c 19y		645	267	4c 8m 19y		704	1620	38c 14m 19y 2k

Swatch	Code	BM No.	CMYK	Swatch	Code	BM No.	CMYK	Swatch	Code	BM No.	CMYK
	705	1422	22c 9m 11y		764	26	50m 47y		823	1418	39c 14m 8y 1k
	706	1150	7c 20m 23y		765	23	1c 19m 21y		824	1044	8c 17m 27y
	707	1500	19c 15m 25y 1k		766	92	1c 13m 19y		825	1226	11c 30m 29y 2k
	708	1618	19c 6m 11y		767	208	5c 28m 51y 1k		826	257	15c 32m 57y 5k
	709	1047	17c 36m 51y 6k		768	6	67m 64y		827	549	31c 1m 38y
	710	216	7c 31m 64y 1k		769	383	15c 31m 60y 5k		828	1135	3c 14m 19y
	711	263	11c 21m 41y 1k		770	191	2c 15m 28y		829	1417	30c 10m 7y 1k
	712	478	17c 9m 32y 1k		771	287	12c 43m 84y 3k		830	288	3c 8m 24y
	713	1205	6c 31m 30y 1k		772	64	1c 17m 19y		831	850	22c 1m 21y
	714	1211	27c 61m 63y 28k		773	3	38m 29y		832	877	6c 8m 11y
	715	205	4c 11m 23y		774	84	65m 73y		833	1502	31c 27m 42y 7k
	716	438	28c 13m 34y 2k		775	354	21m 74y		834	1395	22c 19m 3y
	717	391	15c 28m 75y 5k		776	307	38m 73y		835	52	4c 33m 26y 1k
	718	699	52c 27m 45y 17k		777	1070	16c 43m 56y 5k		836	645	27c 1m 20y
	719	1207	12c 41m 41y 3k		778	157	20m 34y		837	1317	2c 17m 11y
	720	1165	10c 29m 28y 1k		779	43	3c 21m 16y		838	591	54c 37y
	721	1410	23c 12m 11y		780	183	2c 8m 20y		839	523	26c 27m 50y 6k
	722	1242	16c 31m 23y 2k		781	289	2c 12m 30y		840	50	2c 18m 17y
	723	1452	28c 23m 19y 2k		782	113	2c 11m 22y		841	347	1c 14m 48y
	724	458	30c 11m 26y 1k		783	316	1c 9m 28y		842	394	7c 5m 37y
	725	142	16m 35y		784	117	2c 38m 47y		843	393	6c 5m 29y
	726	17	29m 25y		785	335	20m 74y		844	374	4c 14m 36y
	727	464	22c 10m 23y 1k		786	291	1c 22m 54y		845	1261	8c 18m 13y
	728	69	1c 59m 61y		787	557	39c 2m 64y 1k		846	1354	6c 38m 6y 1k
	729	669	60c 31y		788	331	1c 8m 30y		847	1286	13c 69m 46y 3k
	730	115	1c 21m 32y		789	743	38c 16y		848	1597	27c 13m 18y 1k
	731	940	10c 12m 22y		790	597	27c 19y		849	402	14c 6m 48y 1k
	732	794	44c 12y		791	803	82c 16m 20y 6k		850	468	51c 32m 54y 23k
	733	160	35m 59y		792	600	74c 9m 54y 2k		851	513	3c 15m 27y 1k
	734	544	39c 18m 66y 11k		793	167	1c 46m 66y		852	402	14c 6m 48y 1k
	735	392	21c 33m 83y 11k		794	681	31c 3m 22y		853	727	92c 22m 45y 13k
	736	599	60c 40y		795	370	4c 25m 68y 1k		854	38	7c 36m 25y 1k
	737	1136	5c 22m 26y 1k		796	666	31c 21y		855	764	29c 1m 12y
	738	390	9c 23m 62y 2k		797	641	57c 12m 42y		856	400	9c 5m 32y
	739	436	22c 7m 25y		798	774	76c 8m 24y 2k		857	880	6c 6m 9y
	740	278	8c 32m 71y 1k		799	647	52c 1m 33y		858	967	6c 5m 12y
	741	1069	14c 37m 48y 4k		800	500	22c 15m 36y 1k		859	863	17c 8m 17y
	742	446	53c 29m 55y 23k		801	778	39c 12y		860	945	11c 13m 24y
	743	429	21c 6m 31y		802	1111	13c 43m 57y 3k		861	617	23c 1m 19y
	744	674	38c 1m 22y 1k		803	1601	48c 32m 34y 14k		862	979	40c 42m 52y 22k
	745	243	22c 27m 41y 4k		804	418	33c 5m 77y 1k		863	621	62c 3m 44y 1k
	746	404	17c 15m 79y 4k		805	659	31c 20y		864	545	43c 21m 67y 15k
	747	711	58c 16m 34y 8k		806	427	47c 16m 80y 10k		865	773	64c 2m 19y
	748	165	1c 25m 43y		807	889	1c 19m 13y		866	776	93c 24m 30y 20k
	749	387	2c 9m 30y		808	843	24c 2m 18y		867	570	36c 1m 38y
	750	1459	24c 16m 19y 1k		809	1297	1c 50m 30y		868	774	76c 8m 24y 2k
	751	434	51c 29m 77y 35k		810	399	11c 23m 97y 3k		869	820	31c 6m 9y
	752	304	14m 36y		811	759	71c 28y		870	824	71c 27m 15y 14k
	753	866	21c 4m 14y		812	891	3c 8m 14y					
	754	334	16m 61y		813	873	12c 5m 11y					
	755	487	31c 21m 48y 6k		814	1450	12c 10m 12y					
	756	424	26c 3m 43y 1k		815	854	15c 3m 22y					
	757	572	54c 3m 59y 1k		816	1072	6c 18m 24y					
	758	556	32c 1m 51y		817	386	3c 7m 25y					
	759	324	10m 36y		818	688	35c 9m 24y 1k					
	760	312	20m 50y		819	1523	26c 28m 40y 5k					
	761	299	31m 71y		820	875	21c 6m 13y					
	762	772	44c 14y		821	1667	27c 4m 15y					
	763	202	3c 38m 69y 1k		822	388	3c 12m 38y					